D1032330

A fuller understanding of

the paintings at the Orsay Museum

A fuller understanding of the paintings at the Orsay Museum

Courbet, Manet, Renoir, Monet, Degas, Van Gogh, Gauguin...

Françoise Bayle

art lys

M'O

Cover: Vincent Van Gogh, *Starry Night*, 1888,
oil on canvas, 72.5 x 92 cm
pages 8-9: musée d'Orsay, central aisle

Editorial co-ordination: Séverine Cuzin-Schulte
Picture research and editorial follow-up: Karine Barou
Graphic design: Antoine Maiffret
PAO : Catherine Enault and Hervé Delemotte
Production: Pierre Kegels
Photogravure: Imag'in (Vern-sur-Seiche, France)

ISBN: 978-2-85495-402-9

Foreword

This new publication on the collections of paintings at the Musée d'Orsay is not merely one more among the already numerous books inspired by the beauty and richness of the works of art. It takes a truly different, dual approach. It is a genuine guide that proposes both chronological pages, and also theme-based comparisons where the eyes of the various painters meet, sometimes glaringly.

This book thus naturally reviews the great movements in the history of painting between 1848 and 1914, succeeding one another or rubbing shoulders with one another with almost every new decade. As they turn the pages, readers will thus find the great figures of its history in commentaries that retrace the highlights of the artistic life of the time.

But the chronological approach to the works and to the painters is combined with a new, theme-based approach whereby the works are gathered together around common subjects to show either their differences or their similarities. This instructive and sometimes surprising approach brings out the extraordinary vitality of the paintings, and offers greater understanding of the issues that fired the painters and that stirred up the minds around memorable battles.

We hope this dual approach will encourage readers to return to the collections of paintings at the Musée d'Orsay with new eyes and new curiosity.

Contents

expositions

expositions

Thomas Couture, Jean-Léon Gérôme and Rosa Bonheur

Academic painting

Thomas Couture, *Romans of the Decadence*, 1847, oil on canvas, 472 x 772 cm, Salon of 1847

Despite being so different, these pieces are hugely successful. *The Romans of the Decadence* brings together all the criteria required for a history painting, which is still the noblest genre: the literary subject, the format, the grasp of space. Nevertheless, Thomas Couture (1815-1879) wished to denounce the moral decadence of France during the reign of Louis Philippe, the "citizen-king", through a historical satire. Couture embodies what is known as eclecticism since his work consists of a mixture of different elements borrowed from his most diverse predecessors – Veronese and Raphael, to name but a few –, but he would ultimately have his greatest effect on painting as a teacher: Puvis de Chavannes and Manet would spend many years in his studio where, contrary to numerous theories, he developed a non-academic form of teaching, encouraging his pupils to paint in the open air and to use pure colour! This piece by Rosa Bonheur (1822-1899) was commissioned by the State in 1848. The artist painted animals her whole life and even set up her studio in the Château de By, near to the forest of Fontainebleau, so as to be able to study them from life. Although the theme suggests Realist inspiration, its precise, descriptive construction is traditional and academic. Showered with honours – she became the first woman Officer of the Legion of Honour and was appointed director of the École impériale de dessin –, in her lifetime, Rosa Bonheur achieved success reaching beyond the boundaries of France.

Jean-Léon Gérôme, *Young Greeks and Fighting Cocks* or *The Cockfight*, 1846, oil on canvas, 143 x 204 cm, Salon of 1847

Rosa Bonheur, *Ploughing in the Nivernais Region: first dressing*, 1849, oil on canvas, 134 x 260 cm, Salon of 1849

Jean-Auguste-Dominique Ingres, Amaury-Duval and Hippolyte Flandrin

Classicism yet again and again

Amaury-Duval,
The Annunciation, 1860,
oil on canvas, 170 x 125 cm

Since Ingres was born in 1780, most of his paintings are in the Louvre. However, the painter had a very long life and died in 1867, hence his later works are kept at the Musée d'Orsay along with canvases by his many disciples. It was during the World Fair of 1855 that Ingres became consecrated, just like that other artistic genius, Delacroix, his eternal rival, one embodying Neoclassicism and the other, Romanticism. A taste for Antiquity, precision of line and the supremacy of drawing remained sound values for Ingres and his disciples, even though the Master often took liberties with anatomical forms. His disciples, for example Hippolyte Flandrin (1809-1864) and Amaury-Duval (1808-1885), achieved particular renown in sacred art and portraiture. Flandrin was to immortalise the high society of the Second Empire. This neoclassical inspiration would continue in academic painting throughout the 19th century, with artists such as Cabanel and Bouguereau. Supported by the official Salons, it was greatly criticised by the defenders of the new trends in painting, Realism and Impressionism.

Hippolyte Flandrin,
Prince Napoleon,
1860, oil on canvas, 117 x 89 cm

Jean-Auguste-Dominique Ingres,
Venus in Paphos, 1852-1853,
oil on canvas, 91.5 x 70.5 cm

Eugène Delacroix and Théodore Chassériau

Romanticism: Colour and the Orient

Eugène Delacroix,
The Puma, also known as *Lioness Watching Her Prey*, 1859, oil on wood, 41 x 30.5 cm

"For me, Romanticism is the most recent and most current expression of beauty", wrote Baudelaire in 1846, Delacroix's (1798-1863) most famous supporter, who perceived him as "the most evocative of all painters, whose work is the most thought-provoking". It was again Baudelaire, one of the few critics to have defended the finished canvas of *The Lion Hunt* at the World Fair of 1855, who spoke of a "real explosion of colour... Never before have more beautiful or more intense colours reached the very soul through the eyes." Chassériau (1819-1856), originally influenced by Ingres who had taken him into his studio at a very young age, then turned to Delacroix, his master's rival, drawn by his pictorial subject matter and colours. He too was attracted by the Orient, a favourite theme of the Romanticists: "There, everything is large, rich and fertile, like in the Middle Ages, that other sea of poetry," wrote Victor Hugo in the preface to *Les Orientales*. In 1846, Chassériau travelled to Algeria. In *The Tepidarium*, inspired by the public baths excavated in Pompeii two decades earlier, the artist "seems to reconcile, in a single moment, the two rival schools of drawing and colour. Here is a pure colourist, a perfect colourist... in whose drawing no flaws can be found" according to the words of the press.

Eugène Delacroix, *The Lion Hunt*, sketch from 1854,
oil on canvas, 86 x 115 cm

Théodore Chassériau, *The Tepidarium, a room where the women of Pompeii came to relax and dry themselves after bathing*, 1853,
oil on canvas, 171 x 258 cm, Salon of 1853

Camille Corot, Théodore Rousseau and Jules Dupré

The landscape painters: Corot and the Barbizon School

Théodore Rousseau,
An Avenue, Forest on Adam's Island,
1846-1849, oil on canvas,
101 x 82 cm, Salon of 1849

Jules Dupré,
The Lock Gate, circa 1855-1860,
oil on canvas, 51 x 69 cm

Camille Corot,
Morning, Dance of the Nymphs,
1850-1851, oil on canvas,
98 x 131 cm, Salon of 1850-1851

From the 1850s, Corot (1796-1875) turned towards a more evocative and lyrical style of painting: his landscapes painted with a vibrant, light touch, in a muted palette, would henceforth bathe in a dream-like hazy atmosphere. "Let feeling alone be your guide," wrote Corot on a page of an album. "Reality is a part of art; feeling is the finishing touch." Several painters of the same period, but younger than Corot's generation, wanted to escape urban civilisation, which they found inhuman, and discover authentic nature. From the 1830s-1840s, they settled in Barbizon, a village on the edge of the forest of Fontainebleau – Corot would sometimes paint with them. The painters, Théodore Rousseau, Constant Troyon, Narcisse Diaz de La Peña, Jules Dupré, Jean-François Millet, Charles Daubigny... adopted an original approach in that they painted the most "natural" landscapes possible directly from the subject, rather than in the studio, in which they would attempt to render incessant variations of light. They all had a taste for thick, highly triturated material, sometimes slightly heavy and dark, which they would develop over the years into lighter, more broken brushstrokes bringing them closer to the technique that would be adopted by the Impressionists. Bazille, Monet and Renoir were frequent visitors to Barbizon.

Jean-François Millet

The "painter of peasants"

Jean-François Millet (1814-1875), who has been described as the "painter of peasants", began by painting numerous portraits. *The Winnower*, shown at the Salon of 1848, his first monumental pastoral figure, amazed and captivated the Republican sympathisers – it was 1848. This piece had "everything that was needed in order to exasperate the bourgeois," wrote Théophile Gautier. How could a working man of the people become the central subject of a painting? Thus began a period in which Millet, having moved to Barbizon in 1849, painted peasants and their labours. Approximately ten years later, in *The Angelus*, a monumental piece in spite of its modest size, Millet evoked not only the daily labours of the peasants, but also the unchanging rhythms of this simple life, giving his figures an eternal character. "I painted *The Angelus* by remembering how, when working in the fields in the past, on hearing the bells my grandmother would always make us stop work to say the angelus for the "lost souls", with such piety and our hats in our hands," he wrote in a letter in 1865, in which nostalgia prevailed over Realism.

Jean-François Millet,
The Little Shepherdess,
1858-1860, oil on canvas,
32.5 x 25 cm

Jean-François Millet,
The Angelus, 1857-1859,
oil on canvas, 55.5 x 66 cm

Jean-François Millet,
The Winnower, 1866-1868, oil on wood,
79.5 x 58.5 cm, replica with a variation
on the painting shown at the Salon of 1848
(London, National Gallery)

The Gleaners, as perceived by Breton and Millet

Jules Breton,
The Gleaners Return,
1859, oil on canvas, 90 x 176 cm,
Salon of 1859

Painted two years apart, these two "realist" pieces, which more or less illustrate the same theme, are actually quite different. Jules Breton (1827-1906) portrays an idyllic vision of rural life: at the end of the day, the gleaners' faces show no sign of fatigue, and their sheaves are almost too plentiful given the conditions under which the law allowed the poor to collect ears of corn remaining in the stubble before sunset. Jean-François Millet (1814-1875) depicts his gleaners still at work, with bent backs, anonymous faces absorbed in their labours, in low-angled light which emphasises the gestures of the worn-out peasant women, like a single woman perceived at successive stages of her work. The first was a great success, but the second was highly criticised: "Through austerity in crudeness and simplification in abstinence, Millet's peasants thus return, by degrees, to a savage existence." wrote one of Millet's most hostile critics.

Jean-François Millet,
The Gleaners,
1857, oil on canvas, 83.5 x 111 cm,
Salon of 1857

Gustave Courbet

A realist painter or "defender of the ugly"?

Gustave Courbet,
Burial at Ornans,
1849-1850, oil on canvas, 315 x 668 cm,
Salon of 1850-1851

The *Burial at Ornans*, shown at the Salon of 1850-1851, gave rise to criticism claiming that Courbet (1819-1877), a practically self-taught painter, had taken a simple detail of everyday life and raised it to the level of a historical scene using a scale disproportionate to the triviality of the subject. Furthermore, some found the realism of the portraits intolerable. It is ugly because it is real, because it is true: this landscape of Ornans in the Franche-Comté region, the painter's homeland, but also all the inhabitants of the village who posed for this painting by Courbet, christened "the defender of the ugly" by his disparagers. Even the priest is ugly! A few years later, in 1855, *The Painter's Studio* was shown to the public, not at the World Fair which had rejected some of his paintings, but in a temporary pavilion, the "Realism Pavilion" which he had built opposite the official venue and where he had hung approximately forty pieces of work. There was a charge for admission and a catalogue was published, the foreword of which resembled a Realism manifesto. Nevertheless, Courbet, objecting to the Realist label, thus resumed his artistic approach: "My aim is to convey the morals, ideas and an image of my time, according to my own judgement, not only as a painter but as a man, in a word, to create living art". Through his desire to choose subjects of his time and totally rejecting idealism, Courbet led the way for Impressionism.

Gustave Courbet,
The Painter's Studio. A real allegory summing up seven years of my artistic and moral existence, 1854-1855, oil on canvas, 361 x 598 cm

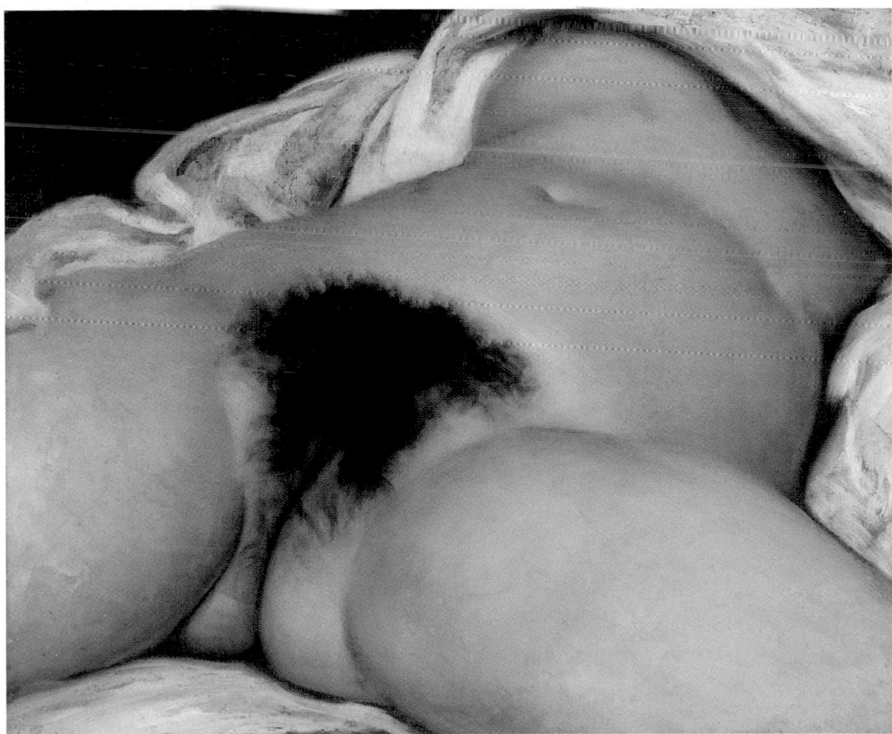

Gustave Courbet,
Origin of the World,
1866, oil on canvas, 46 x 55 cm

Edgar Degas

"Draw lines, young man..."

Edgar Degas, *The Bellelli Family*, 1858-1867, oil on canvas, 200 x 250 cm

Descended, like Manet, from the Parisian bourgeoisie, Degas (1834-1917) was classically trained in the studio of an ardent disciple of Ingres, and then perfected his skills through several trips to Italy – it was there that some of his family, on the paternal side, lived – where he formed a real friendship with Gustave Moreau. At the start of his career, Degas mainly produced history paintings and portraits. The latter, in which he often depicted members of his family, reveal his debt to the great masters of the past – Van Dyck, Holbein, Pontormo, Vélazquez and Goya –, but also to Ingres, whom he is said to have met at least once and who supposedly said to him: "Draw lines, young man, lots of lines, either from memory or from life. That is how you will become a good painter." In *The Bellelli Family*, which he began painting in his aunt's apartment in Florence, his uncle, relegated to the edge of the painting, turns his back with a sullen face, while his aunt poses as if for an official portrait. Each one seems separate in this family with a heavy, solemn atmosphere. Faced with this piece, it is not easy to imagine the rest of Degas' work, which would be linked to the Impressionists and would soon draw its subjects from modern life. He would never abandon the portrait genre, but instead would later paint those around him – critics, writers, collectors, painters, musicians and bankers.

Edgar Degas, *War Scene in the Middle Ages,*
1865, paint mixed with spirits on paper re-mounted
on canvas, 81 x 147 cm

Edgar Degas, *Semiramis Building Babylon,*
circa 1860-1862, oil on canvas, 150 x 258 cm

A theme for two painters, the picnic

Claude Monet,
The Picnic, 1865-1866,
central part of a composition
damaged by damp and then cut
out by the artist,
oil on canvas, 248 x 217 cm

Édouard Manet,
The Picnic,
1863, oil on canvas,
208 x 264 cm,
Salon des Refusés of 1863

In 1863, the jury proved so strict during the selection of work for the official Salon that Emperor Napoleon III came to judge the quality of the rejected work for himself and decided that they would be exhibited in a wing of the industrial design pavilion. Although certain artists preferred to collect their work, others, such as Manet, Pissarro, Jongkind and Whistler, found their work on the walls of the Salon des Refusés. Manet's *Picnic*, then known as *Bathing*, aroused both scandal and laughter. What was this naked woman doing, sitting on the grass in the undergrowth with two men in suits? Nothing. The mythological subject inherited from the old masters had disappeared, and had been replaced by a genre scene in a format which, until then, had been reserved for history paintings. Furthermore, Manet had painted this piece in an almost casual manner, with large flat colours, without bothering to incorporate the figures into the space of the undergrowth, simply brushed on like scenery. "Manet will have talent when he learns to draw and use perspective," wrote a critic. Two years later, as a tribute to the painting, the young Monet took up the same theme and asked his new artist friends to pose for him, arranging figures in spontaneous poses on his canvas using large coloured brushstrokes, with the play of light on the blanket, a face or foliage. With this painting, produced in his studio from sketches drawn from life, Monet signed a real manifesto for painting in the open air and tried to achieve something which would become the concern of future Impressionists, as Émile Zola explained: "placing life-size figures in a landscape".

Claude Monet,
The Picnic, 1865-1866,
left part of a composition
damaged by damp and then cut out by the artist,
oil on canvas, 418 x 150 cm

Camille Corot

Landscapes and figures

Camille Corot,
The Clearing, Memory of Ville-d'Avray,
circa 1872, oil on canvas, 100 x 134 cm

Camille Corot, *Dance of the Nymphs,*
circa 1860-1865, oil on canvas, 47 x 77.5 cm

"Nymphs dancing in a ring... Is this not you whom Corot saw in rhythmical flight in a ballet at the Opera? Sylph-like ballet dancers, the painter's eye stole you away for his own use; you are the very soul of his landscape" (Étienne Moreau-Nélaton). Nymphs, shepherds and shepherdesses pirouette or dream in the undergrowth bathed in mist and haze, in green and brown monochromes which would be incessantly criticised, and even described as "dirty sponge marks" to evoke the silvery foliage. However, although Corot is mainly known for his landscapes, throughout his life he secretly painted figures which he had never dared show to the public – apart from one. These were above all women, real or imaginary, which he captured in nostalgic reverie: averted, distant gazes; melancholic, pensive faces tinged with unfathomable sadness. These pieces finally made their appearance at the Salon d'Automne of 1909, fascinating Degas then, later, the Cubists and Braque.

Camille Corot,
Corot's Studio, Young Woman Deep in Thought, Holding a Mandolin,
circa 1865, oil on canvas, 56 x 46 cm

Two nudes painted the same year: 1863

Alexandre Cabanel,
The Birth of Venus,
1863, oil on canvas, 130 x 225 cm,
Salon of 1863

This is a classic theme, and the two painters drew their inspiration from their illustrious predecessors: Cabanel (1823-1889) from Titian's *Triumph of Galatea*, and Manet (1832-1883) from the *Urbino Venus* by the same painter and Goya's *Naked Maja*. Nevertheless, the first piece, "exquisitely tasteful", had tremendous success at the Salon – Napoleon III decided to purchase it instantly –, whereas the second piece, shown at the Salon two years later, caused a new scandal. Cabanel's Venus, whose smooth, porcelain-like naked body is borne by the waves, is escorted by pink, chubby *putti*. Her head tilted back, she offers herself up, admittedly, languishing. However, she incarnates the ideal of feminine beauty, and her eroticism has the advantage of being discreet and concealed by the mythological subject. This is a heroic nude! Manet's Olympia, painted from a model named Victorine Meurent, watches the onlooker and flaunts her profession, the name of which ought not be spoken – prostitution. To those who described Olympia as "tainted" or the "yellow-bellied odalisque", Zola would reply: "I, myself, know that you have admirably succeeded in creating a work of art, a masterpiece... you have vividly conveyed the truth of light and shadow, the reality of the objects and creatures, in a unique language." The same Zola had described Cabanel's Venus thus: "The goddess, drowning in a river of milk, looks like a delightful lorette [a lady of easy virtue], not made of flesh – that would be indecent – but rather a sort of pink and white almond paste!"

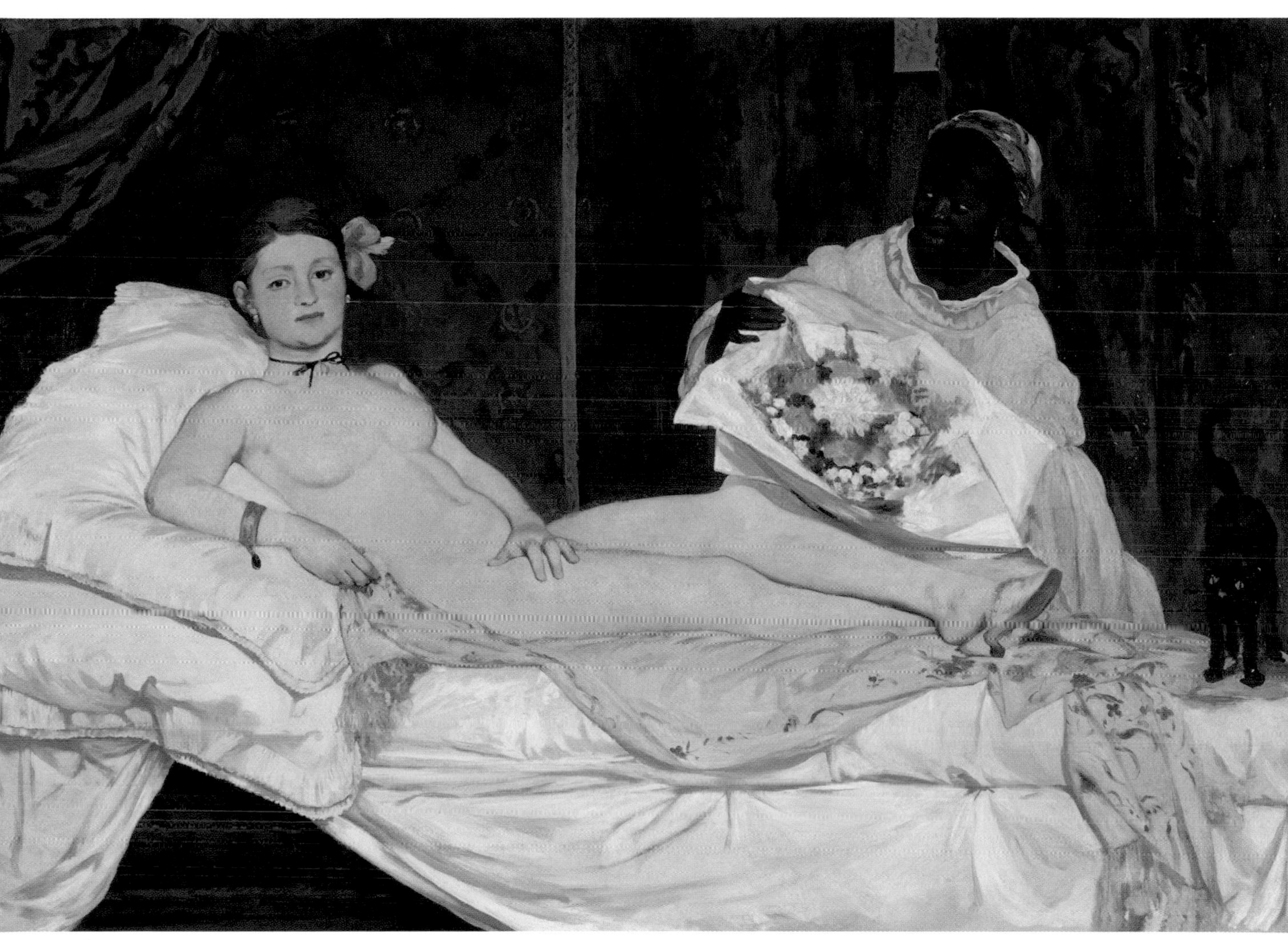

Édouard Manet,
Olympia,
1863, oil on canvas, 130.5 x 190 cm,
Salon of 1865

Édouard Manet

"Don Manet y Courbetos y Zurbarán de Los Batignolles"

Édouard Manet,
Lola of Valence,
1862, oil on canvas,
123 x 92 cm

Manet (1832-1883) may have discovered Spanish painting at the Louvre, as a child, in the magnificent collection of over four hundred and fifty paintings which Baron Taylor had built up for Louis-Philippe, and which had been returned to the exiled monarch after the collapse of the July Monarchy. The painters on display were Greco, Velázquez, Zurbarán, Murillo and Goya... In the 1860s, Manet broadened his Spanish artistic culture: he probably visited the famous Pereire collection, and travelled to Spain. In 1862, a Spanish ballet company appeared in Paris, and the painter invited the dancers to pose for him: Lola of Valence was a member of the company. In this canvas, the painter went so far as to produce an amazing piece of painting, particularly on the dancer's heavily trimmed skirt, with daubs of red, yellow and green. His broken and free brushstrokes caused a real scandal. On that occasion, the painter was ironically re-named "Don Manet y Courbetos y Zurbarán de Los Batignolles" (Manet's studio was situated at 34 du boulevard des Batignolles, and it was at number 11, Grande-Rue des Batignolles, that painters and writers would meet in the Café Guerbois). Spain and its painters would forever remain present in Manet's work: Goya in *The Balcony*, but also Velázquez on several occasions. While staying in Madrid, Manet wrote about the latter: "The trip has been worth it for him alone... He is the painter of painters. I was not surprised, but delighted by his work."

Édouard Manet,
Bullfight, 1865-1866,
oil on canvas, 90 x 110,5 cm

Édouard Manet,
Angelina, 1865,
oil on canvas, 92 x 73 cm

Honoré Daumier

From lithography to painting

Honoré Daumier,
Crispin and Scapin, also known as *Scapin and Sylvester*,
circa 1864, oil on canvas,
60.5 x 82 cm

Honoré Daumier,
Don Quixote and the Dead Mule,
1867, oil on canvas,
132.5 x 54.5 cm

Honoré Daumier (1808-1879), from an extremely humble background, practised various minor trades before joining a printing firm as an apprentice: he then became acquainted with lithography, which he practised his entire life and would be his chief source of income. Politically involved in the July revolution of 1830, he worked with *Charivari* and *La Caricature* as a cartoonist: a victim of censure, he spent several months in prison. His famous busts of members of parliament, the "célébrités du Juste Milieu", "a crackling inferno of ferocity", date from this period. Finally, rather late on at the age of forty, he began painting small canvases which, in contrast to the drawings roughly sketched and delivered each day, were carefully and slowly worked out. However, the urban figures which stand out in very violent contrasts of light and shade seem to be a mere outline. In *The Laundress*, where two figures in the foreground, in the shade, stand out against the lightness of the town, the woman, bent under the weight of the washing, helps the child holding the paddle to climb up the last step. Although Daumier ended his days in poverty and was never understood by the critics, many painters paid tribute to him. In 1846, Delacroix wrote to him saying: "There is not a man that I respect and admire more than you." Degas would collect numerous pieces by Daumier. Van Gogh himself wrote: "People like Daumier should be revered."

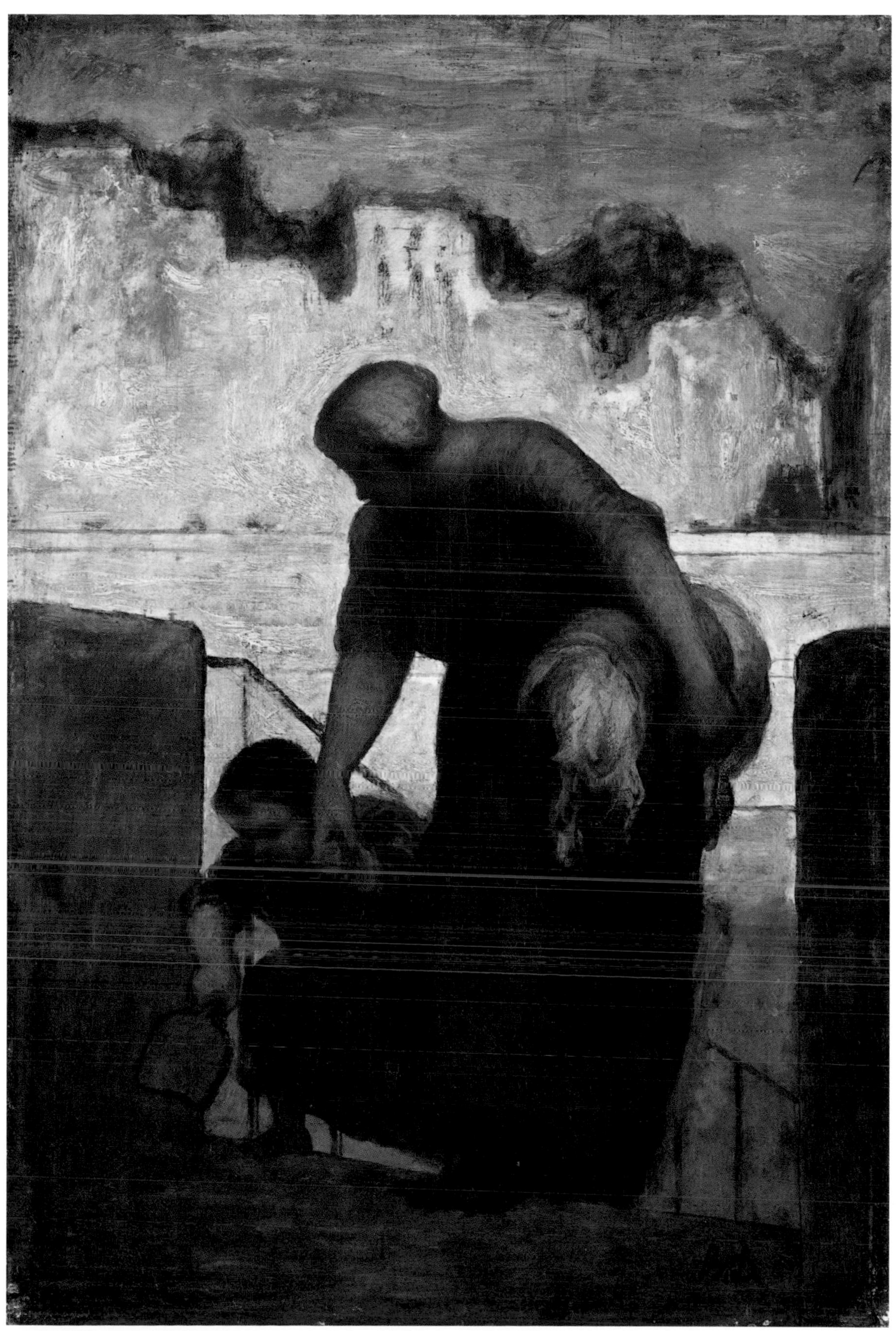

Honoré Daumier, *The Laundress*,
circa 1863, oil on wood, 49 x 33.5 cm

Édouard Manet

"Still-life paintings"

From 1864-1865, Manet (1832-1883) produced "still-life paintings in which the artist [had] scattered fruit and fish on bright white tablecloths, and studies of peonies, which [demonstrate] unquestionably vivid qualities," wrote the art writer Thoré in May 1865. These still-lives are in keep-ing with two traditions: 17th century Spanish and Dutch Vanitas, and Chardin's still-lives. The composition of *Stem of Peonies and Secateurs* resembles Chardin's composition with birds or animals hanging from the wall by their leg, but using peonies instead... *The Vase of Peonies on a Small Pedestal*, combining budding flowers with fallen petals, evokes the inevitable passing of time: "Manet's vase of peonies relates the death of a flower, or, to use a medical term more precise in its cruelty: its agony curve. The movement takes place from right to left, finishing in the centre," wrote the poet André Fraigneau. His brushstrokes are broad, generous and sensual, like in the bouquet held by the black servant woman in *Olympia* or in the still-life of *The Picnic*, giving the peonies their fleshy, luxuriant consistency.

Édouard Manet,
Vase of Peonies on a Small Pedestal,
1864, oil on canvas,
93.2 x 70.2 cm

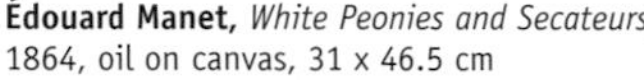

Édouard Manet, *White Peonies and Secateurs,*
1864, oil on canvas, 31 x 46.5 cm

Édouard Manet, *Stem of Peonies and Secateurs,*
1864, oil on canvas, 56.8 x 46.2 cm

Two "Springs" separated not only by a little over a decade

The Spring, represented by a feminine allegorical figure, draws its origin from Greco-Roman mythology, and the two painters attempt to conform to this tradition. Although the critics at the time greatly pondered the degree of reality and the ideal in Ingres' figure, in comparison with Courbet's figure, it was perceived as the quintessential ideal beauty then taught at the École des Beaux-Arts, where students drew by observing copies of antique sculptures. Approximately ten years after Ingres and his pupils had completed *The Spring*, Courbet made a dazzling break with Ingres' idealised, smooth, academic nudes, but also with those shown by conventionalist painters at the official Salons, such as The Birth of Venus by Cabanel. He thus painted the "living French woman" whom Duranty, in *La Nouvelle Peinture* in 1876, prayed would usurp "the Greek marble woman" so esteemed by academic painters. Courbet had portrayed the same living woman as early as 1853, in *Women Bathing*, a large piece which had dared to break with the ideal nude, the most lofty of artistic genres, thus provoking indig-nation and scandal.

Jean-Auguste-Dominique Ingres,
The Spring,
1820-1856,
oil on canvas, 163 x 80 cm

Gustave Courbet, *The Spring,*
1868, oil on canvas, 128 x 97 cm

Édouard Manet

Figures and portraits

Édouard Manet,
The Fife Player,
1866, oil on canvas, 161 x 97 cm,
rejected by the Salon of 1866

Édouard Manet,
The Balcony,
circa 1868-1869, oil on canvas,
170 x 124.5 cm

Édouard Manet,
Portrait of M. and Mme Auguste Manet,
1860, oil on canvas, 111.5 x 91 cm

Manet (1832-1883), in his two paintings which had caused a scandal, *Olympia* and *The Picnic*, had already been criticised for this style of painting using large flat colours, without claiming to convey the perspective or depth of the subject which, since the Renaissance, had been the chief concern of Western painting. In *The Fife Player,* only a thin slip of a shadow and possibly the artist's signature invade the space. Large flat expanses of red, white and black, applied in simplified, broad brushstrokes outline the figure tacked on to a grey background. *The Balcony,* in which Manet gathered a few friends together, was barely more successful. The jovial man looking rather pleased with himself, standing in front of a young boy carrying a tray, is Antoine Guillemet, a landscape painter and a friend of those who would soon come to be described as the "Impressionists". In front of him, standing and a little shy, is Fanny Claus, a young concert violinist who would marry one of Manet's friends. Lastly, sitting and leaning on the balcony with a melancholic expression is the painter Berthe Morisot who was to become one of the Impressionists and marry Manet's brother. Despite the apparent realism of the scene, the three figures seem absent, stilted and mysterious, and once again the painting was perceived as a challenge. The question remains as to whether Manet's parents, who belonged to the cultured upper middle-classes and were also curators, were happy with the path chosen by their son – they had originally intended him to pursue a career in the magistracy and then as a naval officer. It is rather resignation that transpires in this portrait painted by Manet in 1860.

Two society portraits of the Second Empire

Franz Xaver Winterhalter, born in approximately 1805 in Baden, began his career during the reign of Louis-Philippe: he then painted numerous portraits of the royal family and court. He left France for England during the Revolution of 1848, and only returned to France in 1853, where he took up his brushes this time to paint the imperial family – Empress Eugenie was his subject on nine occasions – and the closest members of the court. Although his paintings were very much in vogue in high society, the critics fired a few scathing remarks in his direction. "As for M. Winterhalter, the only thing I may say in his favour is to say nothing at all", according to an article in *L'Artiste*. Although his painting demonstrates unquestionable technical brilliance, it sadly pays more attention to the fabrics than the psychology of his models. The portrait of Mme Louis Joachim Gaudibert, painted in 1868, while Monet was going through a despondent phase, was commissioned by someone whom Monet had described in his letters as "my fan", a merchant from Le Havre, Monet's home town, who had purchased several of his paintings. Monet had already painted life-size women in the open air, in *The Picnic*, but also in an interior setting, since he had exhibited the full-length portrait of his mistress and future wife, Camille, in 1866. Although Monet respects the conventions of the society portrait, which emphasises the social status of the model, he also takes a few liberties, both in the averted gaze of the young woman and in the flowing brushstrokes, vigorously and swiftly painting her silk dress, the floral carpet and the bouquet placed on the pedestal table.

Claude Monet,
Mme Louis Joachim Gaudibert,
1868, oil on canvas, 217 x 138.5 cm

Franz Xaver Winterhalter,
Mme Barbe de Rimsky-Korsakov,
1864, oil on canvas, 117 x 90 cm

Jean-François Millet, Charles-François Daubigny and Narcisse Diaz de La Peña

The Barbizon School, the forerunner of Impressionism?

At the end of 1849, Millet (1814-1875) moved to Barbizon and remained there for practically the rest of his life. From the 1860s onwards, he increasingly painted landscapes, some of which were highly lyrical, such as *Spring*. However, although the Barbizon School to a certain extent led the way for Impressionism, this was rather down to the other Barbizon painters, particularly Charles-François Daubigny (1817-1878) who, in 1857, had a boat built, *Le Bottin*, equipped with a small cabin which he used as a floating studio where he would go to paint his "impressions" from life, gleaned with the currents of the Seine and the Oise. He thus took to the extreme what Corot, followed by the first Barbizon painters, had begun to do when they painted their sketches in the open air: he painted landscapes from life, without reworking them in the studio. Fifteen or so years later, Monet would again take up the idea of a floating studio when he moved to Argenteuil and had a boat built in order to work on the water.

Charles-François Daubigny,
The Arques Valley, circa 1875,
oil on wood, 39 x 67 cm

Charles-François Daubigny,
Sunset over the Oise, 1865,
oil on wood, 39 x 67 cm

Narcisse Diaz de La Peña,
Pond with Kneeling Urchin,
circa 1869-1870, oil on wood,
39 x 55 cm

Jean-François Millet,
Spring, 1868-1873,
oil on canvas, 86 x 111 cm

Eugène Boudin and Johan Barthold Jongkind

On the road to Impressionism

Eugène Boudin,
The Jetty at Deauville,
1869, oil on wood, 23.5 x 32.5 cm

A few kilometres from Honfleur, a modest inn, the Auberge de Saint-Siméon, which had previously welcomed certain Barbizon painters, was often visited by a painter from Honfleur, Eugène Boudin (1824-1898), who painted numerous sketches of landscapes there at the end of the 1850s. "Those amazing studies, so swiftly and accurately sketched from the most inconsistent, the most elusive of things in terms of form and colour, from waves and clouds, always show the date, time and the direction of the wind, written in the margin," wrote Baudelaire in his commentary on the Salon of 1859. In his beach scenes dating from the 1860s, the sparkling, rapidly brushed figures are often merely an excuse to paint the changing light over several hours and the cloudy skies filling two-thirds of the canvas. It was Boudin who, in 1858, took the young Monet to work from life: "I have never forgotten that you were the first one to teach me to understand and to see". However, Monet would also say how he was influenced by the Dutch painter Johan Barthold Jongkind (1819-1891), who spent most of his life in France, whose light, rapid brushstrokes were able to convey the fleeting impression of a vision. "Jongkind looked at my sketches, invited me to come and work with him, explained the whys and wherefores of his style, and, by supplementing the teaching that I had received from Boudin, from that moment became my true master. It is to him that I owe my trained eye...", explained Monet.

Johan Barthold Jongkind,
The Seine and Notre-Dame de Paris,
1864, oil on canvas, 42 x 56.5 cm

Eugène Boudin,
Bathers on the Beach at Trouville,
1869, oil on wood, 31 x 48 cm

Claude Monet

An outdoor painter?

Claude Monet probably remembered the advice that Eugène Boudin had given him a few years previously, in order to convince him to paint landscapes in the open air: “Study, learn to see and paint, do landscapes.” Monet began to paint a large piece directly from life: “A painting of figures, women in light-coloured summer clothes, picking flowers along a garden path; the sun fell straight on to their skirts with dazzling whiteness; the warm shadow of the tree cut across the path, on the dresses bathed in sunlight, a large grey blanket. It had the most peculiar effect”, wrote Zola. However, Monet had probably re-worked each part of the sketch in the studio: “Monet is still here [in Honfleur], working on enormous canvases... he has a canvas almost three metres high with a proportional width: the figures are slightly smaller than life, women dressed in all their finery, picking flowers in a garden, a canvas which he started to paint from life in the open air”, Dubourg wrote to Boudin on 2 February 1867. That same year, when *Women in the Garden* was rejected by the Salon, several artists, including Monet, Renoir, Pissarro, Sisley, Jongkind, Manet and others, decided to send a protest to the Comte de Nieuwerkerke, Superintendent of Fine Art, in order to be granted an exhibition of the rejected works, alongside the official Salon and the World Fair. Their efforts were futile. They then attempted to set up a private exhibition; however, through lack of funds, the project came to an abrupt end. The first Impressionist exhibition would only be organised in 1874.

Claude Monet,
Women in the Garden,
1866-1867,
oil on canvas,
255 x 205 cm,
rejected by the Salon of 1867

Claude Monet,
Farmyard in Normandy,
circa 1863, oil on canvas, 65 x 81.5 cm

Claude Monet,
Garden in Flower at Sainte-Adresse,
circa 1866, oil on canvas, 65 x 54 cm

Claude Monet

The beach, as perceived by Boudin and Manet

Eugène Boudin,
The Beach at Trouville,
1864, oil on wood, 26 x 48 cm

Two painters, two beaches: Trouville and Berck-sur-Mer. The trend had begun with the advent of the new trains which were able to take city-dwellers to the seaside resorts. After Dieppe, the polite society of the Second Empire would meet in Trouville. A painter of seascapes, Boudin was less interested in the sea than the constant variations in the atmosphere and light, so changeable in Normandy, which he conveyed with vibrant, swift brushstrokes. The composition or the forever minuscule figures were really of minor significance. Almost ten years later, during the summer of 1873, Manet painted *On the Beach*, probably from life (there is sand in the paint). Suzanne Manet, the painter's wife, is sitting reading next to her brother-in-law, Eugène – who would marry the painter Berthe Morisot the following year. Unlike Boudin's beach scenes, the two monumental figures situated in the foreground leave little room for the sea and sky, strips of colour running along the top of the painting. Even when painting open-air scenes, Manet remained preoccupied with the composition of his pieces rather than the rendering of the shimmering colours and light, in contrast to those who were still known as "Manet's group" and who, the following year, would become the "Impressionists". Moreover, unlike the Impressionists, Manet, like Degas, would never really be interested in the landscape.

Édouard Manet,
On the Beach,
1873, oil on canvas, 59.5 x 73 cm

Claude Monet

Atmospheric effects

"I am going to the countryside which is so beautiful in these parts, and is perhaps even more pleasant in winter than in summer", Monet wrote to Bazille in December 1868. Unlike Renoir, who simply perceived snow as "a type of mould on the face of nature", Monet, like other Impressionists, would paint numerous snow-covered landscapes, which he often began in the open air and finished in the studio. At the end of the 1860s, although Monet was still interested in the subject – here a meadow, a farm and a magpie in the snow –, he above all wished to convey the effect of the subject: the tranquil silence, the oblique light of a hidden sun, the blue-tinged shadows of the fence falling on the snow, the black magpie perched on the gate as if on the top line of a music score, innumerable variations on white conveying the mellow density of snow. "Winter has come, the Impressionist paints snow. He sees that in the sun the shadows are blue, so he paints blue shadows without a moment's hesitation. And naturally the public laughs", wrote the critic Théodore Duret in 1878. However, Monet above all painted the light in summer, as in *Hôtel des Roches Noires in Trouville*, where the sun, still high in the sky, shines on the promenade by the sea. Hazy silhouettes, captured in a few flowing brushstrokes, pass each other beneath umbrellas, while an elegant man raises his hat in greeting. The flags flap in the wind – one can even hear them.

Claude Monet,
Hôtel des Roches Noires in Trouville,
1870, oil on canvas, 81.1 x 58.3 cm

Claude Monet,
The Magpie, 1869,
oil on canvas, 89 x 130 cm

Claude Monet,
Train in the Countryside,
circa 1870, oil on canvas, 50 x 65 cm

Frédéric Bazille and Paul Guigou

In the light of the South of France

Frédéric Bazille,
Family Gathering,
1867, oil on canvas, 152 x 230 cm,
Salon of 1868

While the painters gathering at Saint-Siméon farm essentially endeavoured to render the damp, misty atmosphere of Normandy, the painters in Provence conveyed the intense Mediterranean light in their canvases. Frédéric Bazille (1841-1870) was born into a large Protestant family in Montpellier which encouraged him in his chosen path. With his passion for painting and music – he organised musical evenings with Gabriel Fauré, also a man of the South –, he trained in Gleyre's studio where he met young artists opposed to academic painting – Monet, Renoir and Sisley. Probably influenced by some of Courbet's canvases, particularly *The Encounter*, painted in 1854, in which the artist had used extremely pronounced contrasts between shade and light, he rapidly found his style in pieces with the sunlight outlining the forms and cutting across the planes. This is observed in *Family Gathering,* in which the artist portrays members of his family on the terrace of the family estate, and demonstrates his great talent as a colourist. Just as he had posed in Monet's *Picnic*, Bazille succeeded in incorporating great figures in a landscape. Paul Guigou (1834-1871), originating from Apt, met Bazille and the Impressionists in Paris at the Café Guerbois. He also conveyed the harsh light of the South in his painting. Both painters would die in the fullness of youth: the former, at the age of twenty-nine, in the battle of Beaune-la-Rolande in 1870; and the latter, at the age of thirty-seven, as a result of a stroke.

Frédéric Bazille,
The Pink Dress or *View of Castelnau-le-Lez,*
1864, oil on canvas, 147 x 110 cm

Paul Guigou,
The Washerwoman,
1860, oil on canvas, 81 x 59 cm

Paul Guigou
1860

Bazille and Renoir, as perceived by each other in 1867

Frédéric Bazille,
Pierre-Auguste Renoir,
1867, oil on canvas,
62 x 51 cm

Many years later, Renoir described his meeting with Bazille to his son. Having left Gleyre's studio and while travelling through Luxembourg, Bazille struck up a conversation with Renoir, claiming that "the great classical compositions are finished. The spectacle of everyday life is more thrilling." When Renoir asked Bazille, "truly elegant, with the elegance of people who make their manservants wear in their new shoes", why he had spoken to him, Bazille retorted: "Your way of drawing; I believe you are somebody." Thus began a friendship, demonstrated by these two portraits. The one painted by Bazille in broad, strong brushstrokes, probably a sketch, shows Renoir in a relaxed pose. The figure of the great Bazille shows the same relaxation, sitting with his legs crossed in front of an easel, whilst painting a still-life, *The Heron*, now at the Musée Fabre in Montpellier. Behind Bazille, *The Cart. Snow-Covered Road in Honfleur* can be seen, painted by Monet in 1867. These pieces thus reveal the bonds of friendship between the young painters since Bazille, wealthy and generous, had often supported his new friends, either by offering them a place in his successive studios – Renoir shared the studio situated on rue Visconti –, or by purchasing their canvases. This is how he acquired *Women in the Garden*, which had been rejected by the Salon of 1867.

Pierre-Auguste Renoir,
Frédéric Bazille,
1867, oil on canvas,
105 x 73.5 cm

Eugène Fromentin, Gustave Guillaumet and Léon Belly

After the romantic Orient, a more naturalist Orient

Following in the footsteps of Delacroix, other painters embarked on the journey to the Orient. Among them, Gustave Guillaumet (1840-1887), also a writer (*Lettres d'un voyageur and Tableaux algériens*), visited Algeria approximately ten times: he then painted the destitute lives of the desert populations, and shared in their day-today existence; some of his canvases, such as *The Sahara*, are bathed in a strange, disturbing atmosphere. A writer, like Guillaumet, but also an art critic and painter, Eugène Fromentin (1820-1876) was inspired uniquely by Algeria and the Sahara, and had a few favourite themes, such as desert convoys or hunting scenes, in which he combined extremely rich colours with such perfection in drawing almost reminiscent of Ingres. Although highly rated – his *Hunting with Falcons in Algeria; the Quarry* was a triumphant success at the Salon of 1863, and he often produced replicas of his canvases –, his work rapidly attracted critics, who denounced his lack of spontaneity and over-worked "style". The work of these travelling painters, who combined a taste for the narrative, and occasionally even drama, with a realist vision, reveals a form of Orientalism changing from a mythical, voluptuous vision of the Orient to a more naturalist perception, in which the painter endeavours to "encounter and study the familiar objects and customs of a people, to penetrate their beliefs and attitudes", as observed by Jacques Thuillier.

Eugène Fromentin,
Hunting with Falcons in Algeria; the Quarry,
1863, oil on canvas, 162 x 118 cm, Salon of 1863

Gustave Guillaumet,
The Sahara, also known as *The Desert*,
1867, oil on canvas, 110 x 200 cm

Léon Belly,
Pilgrims on the Road to Mecca,
1861, oil on canvas, 161 x 242 cm, Salon of 1861

Paul Cézanne

Difficult beginnings

The son of a banker from Aix, Paul Cézanne (1839-1906) had to overcome his father's reluctance in order to paint. He began his legal studies while attending drawing classes. His fellow countryman, Émile Zola, whom he met at an early age and who had moved to Paris, urged him to join him there and embark upon an artistic career. After initially failing the competitive entrance examination for the Beaux-Arts in 1861, Cézanne moved to the capital in 1862. There, he assiduously copied paintings by the great masters at the Louvre – "The Louvre is the book which teaches us how to read", he once said – and frequented the Académie Suisse, a studio where painters worked freely from life models since the professors merely visited each week to correct the work of each student. He was then introduced to Guillaumin, Pissarro, Monet, Renoir, Sisley and Bazille. However, his work attracted sarcastic remarks from his friends: his themes are, in fact, violent, sensual and morbid, and he painted in dark tones, with heavily loaded brushmarks, with powerful chiaroscuro, as shown by *The Magdalene*, executed for the drawing-room of the Jas-de-Bouffan family estate near Aix-en-Provence. The large portrait of his friend, the painter Achille Emperaire, was rejected by the Salon for several reasons: the deformity of the figure – the head is too big, the legs too short, the arms too thin –, but also and, perhaps, mainly due to the way in which the canvas was executed – broad brushstrokes, thick black lines demarcating the contours.

Paul Cézanne,
The Magdalene or Pain,
circa 1868-1869,
oil on canvas, 165 x 125.5 cm

Paul Cézanne,
Uncle Dominique, Barrister-at-Law,
circa 1866, oil on canvas, 63 x 52 cm

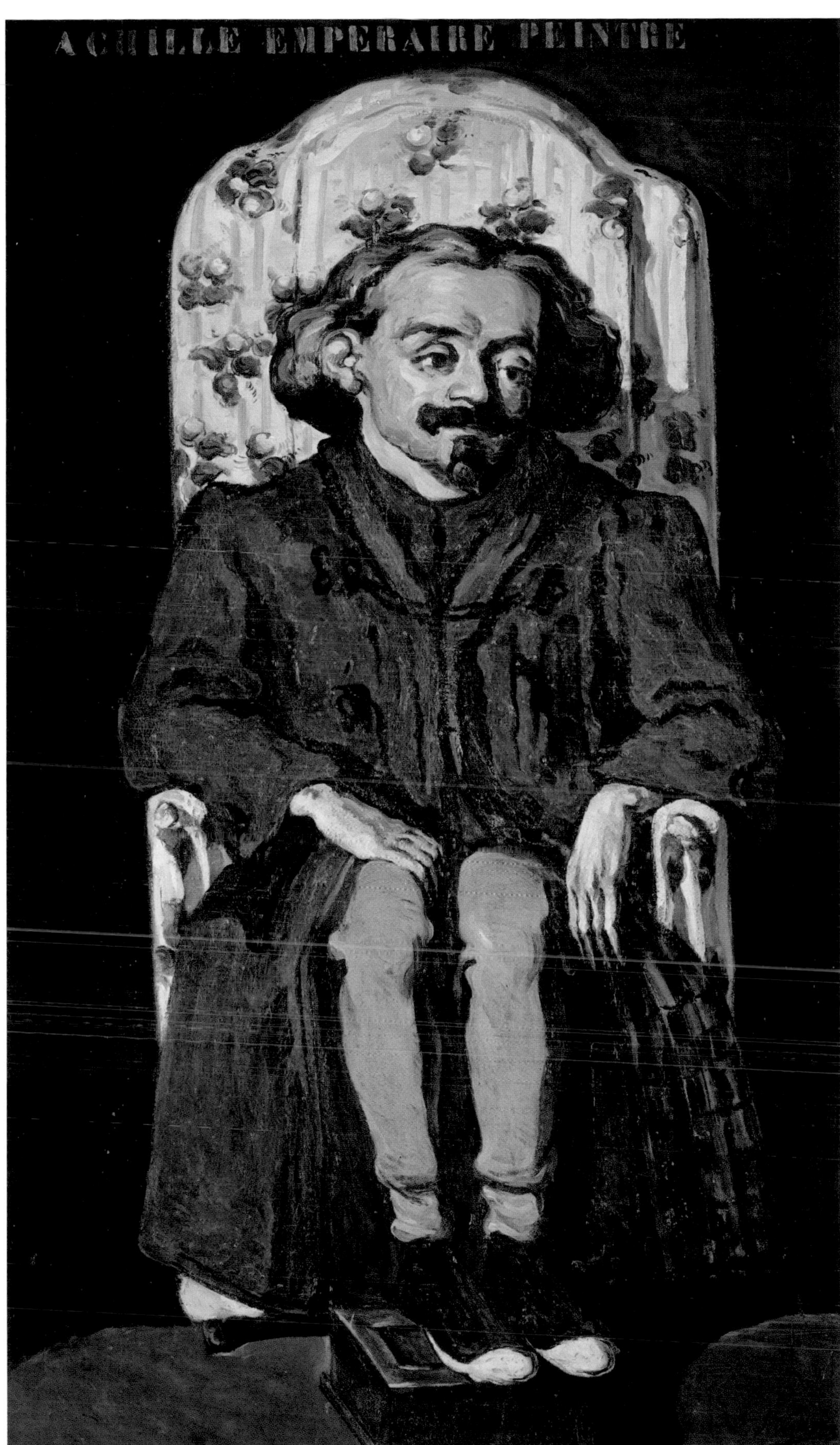

Paul Cézanne,
Achille Emperaire, Painter from Aix,
circa 1869-1870,
oil on canvas,
200 x 120 cm, rejected by the Salon of 1870

Henri Fantin-Latour, Gustave Courbet and Nadar

The role of Baudelaire, the founder of modernity

Henri Fantin-Latour,
Homage to Delacroix,
1864, oil on canvas, 160 x 250 cm,
(detail below, portrait of Baudelaire)

Homage to Delacroix was painted by Fantin-Latour (1836-1904) a year after the death of the romantic master. Fantin-Latour depicts ten men, in a classic composition evoking 17th-century Dutch group portraits – reminiscent of those painted by Frans Hals –, on either side of the portrait of Delacroix, ready to pose as though staring at the lens. They thus paid homage to one who was considered the ancestor of "modern" painting, an idea that would endure: Signac, the theoretician of Neo-Impressionism, entitled his work published in 1899, *D'Eugène Delacroix au néo-impressionnisme*. The painters and critics gathered here include Charles Baudelaire, whose presence is justified on two accounts. Firstly because he was an ardent defender of Delacroix (his study on *L'Œuvre et la vie d'Eugène Delacroix* was published in 1863) and, secondly, because he had defined the idea of modernity at the end of the 1840s: "He will be the painter, the true painter, who will be able to wrest the epic aspect from modern life, and who will be able to make us see and understand, through colour and design, how great and poetic we are in our cravats and shiny boots."

Gustave Courbet,
The Painter's Studio.
A real allegory summing up seven years of my artistic and moral existence,
1854-1855, oil on canvas, 361 x 598 cm
(detail, portrait of Baudelaire)

Félix Tournachon, known as Nadar,
Portrait of Charles Baudelaire seated on a Louis XIII armchair, circa 1855, salt print from a glass negative, 21.2 x 16.1 cm

The "wonderful contemporary", with his cities, his trains, his crowds and his women thus deserves to become the subject of a painting. *Le peintre de la vie moderne* was thus published in 1863, in which he defends the painter Constantin Guys and, beyond that, modernity. "The painter is increasingly led not to paint that which he dreams of, but that which he sees", he adds. This did not necessarily mean that Baudelaire was an ardent ad-mirer of Courbet's Realism, which, for him, lacked "the eternal and the perpetual", that part of the imagination and the supernatural.

Gustave Moreau

Late Romantic or early Symbolist?

The work of Gustave Moreau (1826-1898) drew greatly on the great masters of the Renaissance, whom he first copied at the Louvre, and then discovered during a visit to Italy which lasted almost two years, where he was filled with enthusiasm by the art of Raphael, Leonardo da Vinci and Michelangelo. In *Orpheus*, the somewhat mysterious rocky landscape, the blue-tinged glaciers and the silvery reflections of a river winding its way in the distance are taken straight from the distant landscapes painted by Leonardo. Even though some of Gustave Moreau's paintings were immensely successful – at the Salon of 1866, *Orpheus* was immediately purchased by the State for the Musée du Luxembourg –, the artist seemed stranded between academic painting and "new painting", whether Realism or Impressionism. He generally borrowed his subjects, which were usually complex, from mythology – he would often write a brief note accompanying the titles of his paintings to serve as an explanation. The scholarly observation in his canvases, his rich imagination, his taste for the exotic and the picturesque and the almost applied virtuosity of his brush often gave rise to severe criticism, even from his friends, such as Du Camp who warned him against "this kind of graceful, dainty arrangement which is ornamentation rather than painting". As for Thoré Bürger, a supporter of the Realists, his judgement is final: "the term enigma is befitting for this pretentious, absurd nonsense which the top critics commend under the pretext of the Ideal". However, he did not only have enemies: his most ardent admirers were among the literary circles, the Symbolist and Parnassian poets – Jules Laforgue, José Maria de Heredia and Henri de Régnier – , not forgetting Marcel Proust.

Gustave Moreau, *Jason and Medea,* 1865, oil on canvas, 204 x 115.5 cm

Gustave Moreau, *Orpheus,* 1866, oil on wood, 154 x 99.5 cm

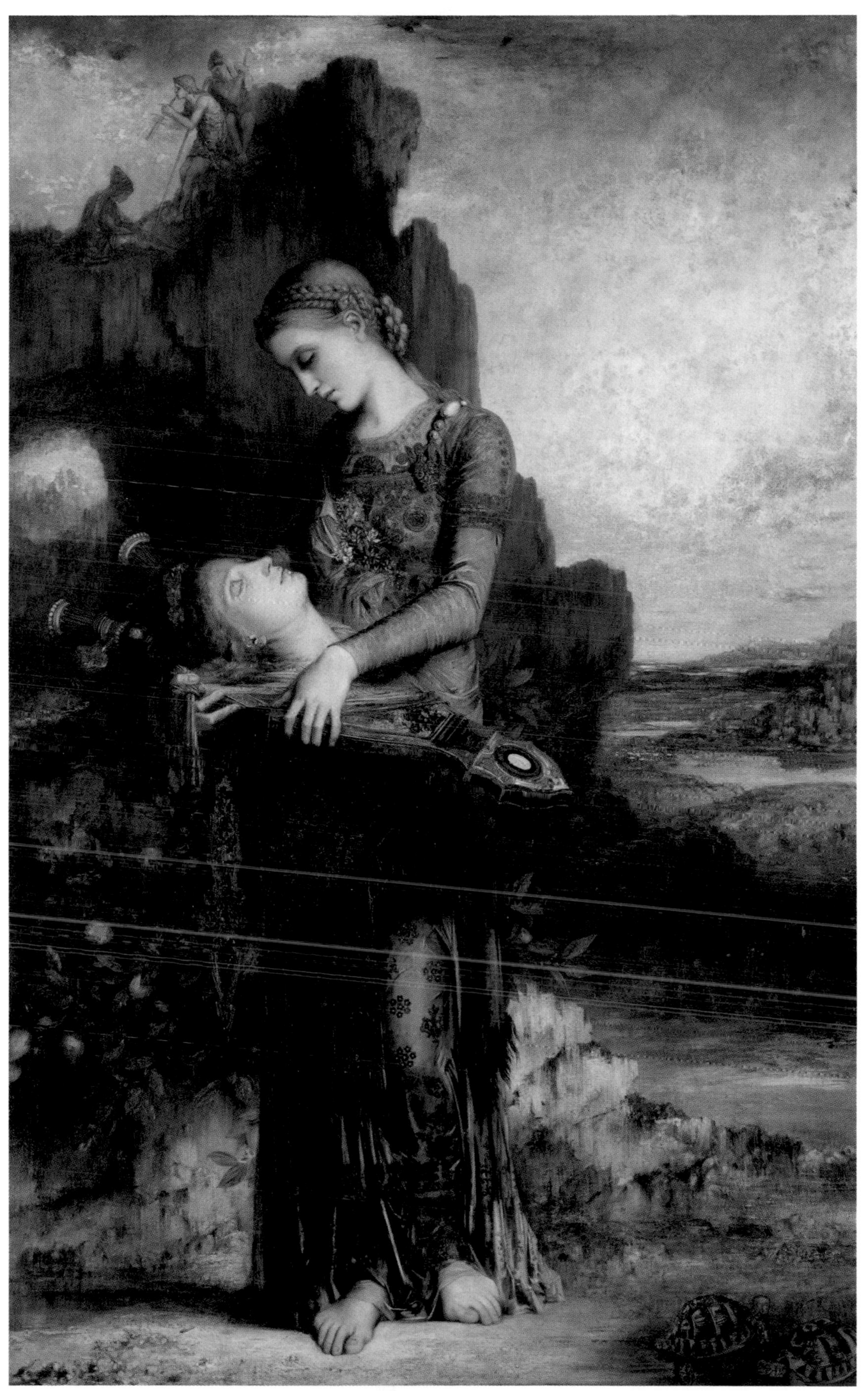

Étretat perceived by two painters: Monet and Courbet

Claude Monet,
Heavy Seas at Étretat,
circa 1868-1869, oil on canvas,
66 x 131 cm

The same subject, the famous Porte d'Aval, caught the attention of both painters, who frequented the Normandy coast during the same period. In Courbet's piece, the only trace of human presence is evoked by the boats run aground on the sand. While, in most of his seascapes painted at Étretat during this period, the sky is overcast with black clouds, here the storm has cleared the atmosphere which has become limpid once again: the sun is warm and the clouds are dispersing. However, the strong element of the composition are the cliffs, the whole texture of the rocks being conveyed, exactly like in his Franche-Comté landscapes. Unlike Courbet, Monet sketched minuscule silhouettes from the back, against the sunlight, on his beach, almost as if looking out for something. According to Jacques-Émile Blanche, after the war of 1914, when Monet was half blind, he wanted to go to Dieppe, one day in November, in order to "contemplate the storm, the raging sea, the menacing clouds". It was this raging sea that he had already depicted, more than forty years previously. "I spend my time outdoors on the shingle in rough weather... and I naturally spend the whole time working...", he then wrote to Bazille. In his painting, the grey cliffs are simplified, whereas the greenish-grey waves and the white foam beneath a leaden sky entirely caught his attention. "For me, a landscape does not exist in itself, since its appearance is constantly changing... The surrounding atmosphere alone gives its qualities to the subject", he wrote. This is how, over the passing years, Monet would finally make the subject disappear.

Gustave Courbet,
The Cliffs of Étretat After the Storm,
1870, oil on canvas, 133 x 162 cm,
Salon of 1870

Ernest Meissonier, Alphonse de Neuville and Édouard Detaille

The war of 1870, as perceived by painters

Alphonse de Neuville,
The Cemetery of Saint-Privat, 18 August 1870,
1881, oil on canvas, 235 x 341 cm, Salon of 1881

In July 1870, Prussia declared war on France, which would end, in January 1871, in French defeat and civil war, the Commune, between the insurrectionary forces and the government. "When my house was invaded by the enemy, I locked myself in my studio where I painted the sketch of Paris. That was my revenge!" related Ernest Meissonier (1815-1891): enlisted in 1870, he remained extremely wounded by the defeat. In this small painting, which is not devoid of a certain epic greatness, he combines real personalities – the catalogue from the Salon of 1884, where the piece was exhibited, identifies several of the figures in the foreground – with allegorical figures: in the top-left of the painting, the ghost of Famine is accompanied by the Prussian eagle, while at the centre of the composition a woman stands, taller than the others, holding the torn French flag, wearing a lion skin on her head, symbolising the city of Paris – echoing the figure of Liberty in Delacroix's *Liberty Guiding the People*. Alphonse de Neuville (1836-1885), also enlisted as a lieutenant in the Engineers, painted the frenzy and desolation of war in this immense fresco: "My desire is to describe our defeats in a way that is honourable to us, and thus give our soldiers a token of respect and, their leaders, encouragement for the future. Whatever anyone says, we were not defeated without glory, and I believe that it is right to show this." Édouard Detaille (1848-1912), a friend of Alphonse de Neuville with whom he painted immense pieces, served his apprenticeship in Meissonier's studio. Like Meissonier, he also served in the war of 1870 and devoted his whole life to military painting. The Impressionists failed to echo these terrible years in their work and, evidently, did not hold this genre in high esteem: Degas, who had a sense of the quip, had described Meissonier as the "giant of the dwarfs"!

Ernest Meissonier,
The Siege on Paris,
1870, oil on canvas, 53.5 x 70.5 cm

Édouard Detaille,
Battle in Villejuif, the Siege on Paris,
19 September 1870,
1870, oil on canvas, 55 x 67 cm

Two studios in Les Batignolles by Henri Fantin-Latour and Frédéric Bazille

Henri Fantin-Latour,
A Studio in Les Batignolles,
1870, oil on canvas, 204 x 273.5 cm,
Salon of 1870

With its hung paintings, armchairs and red tablecloth, Manet's studio, situated at number 34 boulevard des Batignolles, painted by Fantin-Latour (1836-1904), resembles a bourgeois apartment rather than a cluttered artist's studio: here, the studio has been transformed into a place for artists to meet and exhibit their work. Manet, sitting in front of his easel, is in the process of painting the portrait of Zacharie Astruc, critic, painter and sculptor, surrounded by Émile Zola, Edmond Maître, a cultured enthusiast with a love of music, together with other painters – Otto Scholderer, Renoir, Bazille and Monet. Some of these characters also reappear in *The Studio on Rue La Condamine*, by Bazille, even though the identity of certain figures has occasionally been questioned. Renoir, Bazille, Manet, Edmond Maître, and perhaps Zola, Monet and Astruc are nevertheless recognisable. Bazille often painted the studios he frequented: the studio on rue de Fürstenberg in 1865, and the one on rue de Visconti in 1867. As the fashion of painting out of doors developed, the function of the studio changed. Henceforth, painters, with their folding easels and boxes of paint in tubes, would go where they saw fit: "Impressionism cannot exist without tubes of paint", stated Renoir. Evidently the problem of large paintings remained. Monet had to face this problem when he painted *Women in the Garden*: "I had dug a hole in the ground, a sort of ditch, in which I could gradually bury my canvas while I painted the top." There was also the problem of finishing the paintings: the Impressionists practically never admitted that most of their paintings were subsequently re-worked in the privacy of their studios.

Frédéric Bazille,
The Studio on Rue La Condamine,
1870, oil on canvas, 98 x 128 cm

Edgar Degas

Chronicling modern life

Edgar Degas,
The Parade or *Racehorses in front of the Stands,*
circa 1866-1868, paint mixed with spirits on paper re-mounted on canvas, 46 x 61 cm

"I do not have to argue in favour of the cause of modern subjects. This cause was won a long time ago. After the outstanding work by Manet and Courbet, no-one would dare assert that the present time is not worthy of the paint brush", wrote Zola in the commentary for the Salon of 1868. Perfectly illustrating the writer's words, Degas abandoned his history subjects to focus on "modernity". "Degas has become enamoured of modernity... In copying modern life, he has been able to capture its very soul", declared the Goncourt brothers. The races, recently introduced into France by the British, were part of modern life: racecourses were built during that period – as was the Longchamp Racecourse. Even in his exterior scenes, Degas, unlike the Impressionists, was not interested in landscapes: neither topographical precision nor the changing reflections of the light caught his attention. Furthermore, *The Parade* was painted in the studio. Its carefully studied composition nevertheless gives an illusion of reality, similar to the way in which a photographer would capture reality in a brief moment: the horses pass each other on the canvas, one even seems to be walking off the painting. "He is able to paint in such a way that it no longer resembles a composition", wrote the German painter Max Liebermann. In the same way that he painted not the actual race itself, but rather the moments before or after the race, Degas above all painted rehearsals and dance classes, in which once again, like in the racing scenes, it was the movement and various postures of the dancers that he found interesting. At that time, Étienne-Jules Marey, from France, and Edward Muybridge, from the United States, were studying the deconstruction of movement using photography, research which was of great interest to Degas.

Edgar Degas,
Dancer with Bouquet, Curtseying on Stage,
circa 1877, pastel (and gouache?)
on paper glued onto canvas, 72 x 77.5 cm

Edgar Degas,
Ballet Rehearsal on the Stage,
1874, oil on canvas, 65 x 81 cm,
1st Impressionist Exhibition in 1874

Claude Monet and Alfred Sisley

Argenteuil in 1872: Monet settles there, joined by other artists

Claude Monet,
Argenteuil Bridge,
1874, oil on canvas, 60.5 x 80 cm

Alfred Sisley,
The Footbridge at Argenteuil,
1872, oil on canvas, 39 x 60 cm

Claude Monet,
Regatta at Argenteuil,
circa 1872, oil on canvas, 48 x 75 cm

After returning from England and Holland, Monet decided to settle in Argenteuil, and was soon joined by his friends: Renoir, Sisley, and also Manet, who arrived in the summer of 1874, a very rich period for all of the painters. Monet would place his easel on one of the banks of the Seine or work in his famous floating studio. The year he painted *Argenteuil Bridge* marked the official birth of Impressionism, a malicious, scornful neologism created by Louis Leroy, a journalist from Charivari. When the latter visited the exhibition by the "Société anonyme des artistes peintres, sculpteurs, graveurs, etc.", in the photographer Nadar's former studio at 35, boulevard des Capucines, he pondered over Monet's painting, *Impression, Sunrise*: "What does this painting represent? Look in the booklet. — Impression, Sunrise. — Impression, that was certain. I also thought to myself, since I was «impressed», there must be some «impression» in it... And what freedom, what looseness in his technique! Even wallpaper in its embryonic state is more developed than that seascape!" Louis Leroy unwillingly put his finger on the meaning of the title which Monet had chosen for the painting when the catalogue was drawn up: he did not want to paint a seascape of Le Havre, but rather the impression that it left on him. Moreover, the artists, seeing that the critic had – ironically, in spite of himself – understood their intentions, began to describe themselves as "Impressionists".

The Impressionists and water

"I would always want to be by the water", Monet confessed to Gustave Geffroy, "or over the water, and, when I die, I would like to be buried in a buay." In fact, the number of paintings at the Musée d'Orsay speaks for itself: unquestionably, even more so than Sisley – but it is true that Monet's longevity encouraged this –, the "Raphael of the water", as he was described by Manet, loved to paint this element in all its forms: "He is one of the only painters who know how to paint water, without simple transparency, without false reflections", Zola wrote in an article on his Salon of 1868. "With him, the water is alive, deep and, above all, true. It laps around the boats with small greenish waves, broken with white glimmering light, it stretches out in dull blue-green ponds suddenly rippled by the breeze, it lengthens the masts which it reflects breaking their image, its pale, dull tones become enlivened with bright light. This is not the artificial, pure, crystalline water, of armchair seascape painters, this is the still water of the ports strewn with patches of oil, this is the great livid water of the vast, heaving ocean, shaking its dirty foam." The reflections of the water, ever moving, ever changing under the effects of the atmosphere. The technique adopted by the Impressionists, with their fragmented, quivering brushstrokes, this blurredness and sense of incompleteness for which they have been so criticised, matches its transient, fleeting nature. Moreover, it was, in fact, a seascape which lent its name to the Impressionist movement: *Impression, Sunrise*.

Alfred Sisley,
The Boat during the Flood, Port-Marly, 1876,
oil on canvas,
60 x 61 cm

Alfred Sisley,
Flooding at Port-Marly,
1876, oil on canvas,
50,5 x 81 cm

Camille Pissarro,
The Wash-Shed, Port-Marly,
1872, oil on canvas,
46.5 x 56 cm,
4th Impressionist Exhibition, 1879

Claude Monet,
Lily Pond, Harmony of Pinks,
1900, oil on canvas, 89.5 x 100 cm

Claude Monet,
The Rocks of Belle-Île: the Wild Coast,
1886, oil on canvas, 65 x 81.5 cm

Alfred Sisley, *The Regatta at Molesey,*
1874, oil on canvas, 66 x 91.5 cm

Claude Monet, *The Seine at Vétheuil,*
circa 1879-1880, oil on canvas, 43.5 x 70.5 cm

Gustave Caillebotte,
Sailing Boats at Argenteuil,
circa 1888, oil on canvas,
65 x 55.5 cm

Claude Monet,
The Boats. Regatta at Argenteuil,
circa 1874, oil on canvas,
60 x 100 cm

Claude Monet,
Yachts. Argenteuil,
circa 1872, oil on canvas, 49 x 65 cm

Claude Monet,
The Lake at Argenteuil,
circa 1872, oil on canvas,
60 x 80.5 cm

Claude Monet,
Argenteuil Bridge,
1874, oil on canvas, 60.5 x 80 cm

Camille Pissarro and Alfred Sisley

Impressionist landscapes

"I have remained with Sisley the tail end of Impressionism", said Camille Pissarro (1830-1903), who had long given up hope of ever selling his paintings. After having spent his childhood in the Danish colonies in the West Indies, Pissarro ran away to Venezuela to dedicate himself to art. In 1855, his father finally agreed for him to train in Paris. Pissarro then worked with "father Corot", followed by Daubigny and Courbet. Towards the end of the 1860s, he was a regular at the Café Guerbois where the future Impressionists used to meet – he was the only one to take part in all eight Impressionist exhibitions. He then developed his own personal style, less interested in the changes in light and the sky than in the geometrical structure of the landscapes – his main subject –, which is exactly what Cézanne would do. During that time, his successive places of residence provided the subject of his canvases. In *Red Roofs*, horizontal lines marked by the roofs of the houses and the hill are intersected by the diagonals of the gables. The fragmented brushstrokes, not at all evanescent, are rather impasted in certain places. Often, a small silhouette walks along a road around which the lines of the painting are arranged. Like Bazille, Monet and Renoir, Alfred Sisley (1839-1899) was a regular visitor to Gleyre's studio, who recommended painting quick sketches from life. Sisley devoted himself, more so than Pissarro, to exclusively rural landscapes of the outskirts of Paris: his light, clear brushstrokes subtly convey the innumerable variations in the atmosphere, the sky and the light. The British landscape painters at the beginning of the century had an undeniable influence on Sisley: even though he spent almost his entire life in France, Sisley, a British citizen, trained in England and returned there regularly. Sisley ended his days, spurned and unrecognised, in the most cruel poverty.

Camille Pissarro,
Hill of the Hermitage, Pontoise,
1873, oil on canvas, 61 x 73 cm

Alfred Sisley,
Road Leading to La Machine, Louveciennes,
1873, oil on canvas, 54.5 x 73 cm

Camille Pissarro,
The Road to Louveciennes,
1872, oil on canvas, 60 x 73.5 cm

Camille Pissarro,
Red Roofs, Corner of the Village, Effects of Winter,
1877, oil on canvas, 54.5 x 65.6 cm,
3rd Impressionist Exhibition, 1877

Paul Cézanne

His Impressionist period, Auvers-sur-Oise, 1872

Having worked with Pissarro in Pontoise in the spring of 1872, Cézanne accepted his invitation to spend the autumn in Auvers-sur-Oise, near the house of Doctor Gachet, an enlightened collector. He benefited from Pissarro's advice, the latter being one of the few friends who supported him: "We have great expectations for Cézanne, and I have seen a painting with remarkable strength and vigour, which is also at my house. If, as I am hoping, he will stay in Auvers for a while, he will amaze artists who have been too quick to condemn him." Cézanne's art then changed appreciably: he abandoned his original themes, which were often violent, for landscapes, and replaced his dark, heavy style with a light palette and disjointed brushstrokes. These few years are considered Cézanne's Impressionist period. However, unlike the Impressionists whose disjointed, light brushstrokes dissolve forms

Paul Cézanne,
House of the Hanged Man, Auvers-sur-Oise,
1873, oil on canvas, 55 x 66 cm,
1st Impressionist Exhibition, 1874

in the shimmering light and atmosphere, he painted with juxtaposed brushstrokes which he superimposed in places, giving a solid structure to the different elements of the landscape. This is observed in *House of the Hanged Man*, in which the brushstrokes, rather grainy in places, and the geometrical forms – mainly triangles – which arrange the composition around a central point, give the elements of the landscape density and volume. Pissarro was the only other Impressionist who attempted to render volume. The two differ in their way of applying colour. As observed by a farmer who had seen them sitting side by side behind their easels in the Auvers countryside, "M. Pissarro worked using a spotting motion... and M. Cézanne a plastering motion".

Paul Cézanne,
Dr Gachet's House in Auvers,
circa 1872-1873, oil on canvas, 46 x 38 cm

Paul Cézanne,
Crossroad at rue Rémy in Auvers,
circa 1873, oil on canvas, 38 x 45.5 cm

Edgar Degas

The Opera

A letter written by Degas, while staying in New Orleans in 1872, reveals his love for music and the opera: "I really need them! There will be no opera here this winter. Yesterday evening, I went to a rather dismal concert, the first of the year". And in another letter: "The lack of opera is true suffering." As a friend of Emmanuel Chabrier, Degas had probably been introduced to the musical circles by his childhood friend, Ludovic Halévy, whose name is inextricably linked to Henri Meilhac on the librettos for Offenbach's operettas. Degas depicts Ludovic Halévy in the wings of the Opera by the side of Albert Boulanger-Cavé, in *Portraits of Friends on Stage*. With regard to this piece, Halévy wrote in his journal: "Yesterday Degas exhibited two portraits of Cavé and myself. We are both standing in the wings face to face. Me, serious in a frivolous place: that was what Degas wanted to achieve." In *The Orchestra at the Opera*, with Emmanuel Chabrier's head peering over the box, Degas surrounded his friend, Désiré Dihau, bassoonist, whose portrait he had wanted to paint, with other musicians, and also certain close friends. As is often the case in his work, he chose to portray something that is not generally seen: here, the orchestra pit rather than the stage. The composition, which may seem natural, is in fact carefully planned and does not take into account the rules of geometrical perspective. Instead of aspiring to a unique, simultaneous viewpoint, Degas reconstructs that which his gaze deconstructs in several stages. In order to unify the two spaces successively perceived by the eye according to two viewpoints, he uses the head of the double bass, which provides the connection between the orchestra pit and the stage.

Edgar Degas, *The Chorus,* also known as *The Extras,* 1876-1877, pastel on monotype, 27 x 31 cm

Edgar Degas,
Portraits of Friends on Stage, Ludovic Halévy and Albert Boulanger-Cavé, in the wings of the Opera, 1879, pastel, 79 x 55 cm, 4th Impressionist Exhibition, 1879

Edgar Degas,
The Orchestra at the Opera,
circa 1870, oil on canvas, 56.5 x 46.2 cm

Claude Monet

The railway

Claude Monet,
Saint-Lazare Railway Station,
1877, oil on canvas, 75.5 x 104 cm

This year M. Claude Monet... "has exhibited superb interiors of railway stations. One can hear the thundering of the rushing trains, one can see the smoke rolling beneath the vast sheds. That is painting today, in these wonderfully broad modern settings. Our artists must discover the poetry of railway stations, just as their fathers discovered that of the forests and rivers", Émile Zola wrote in *Le Sémaphore de Marseille* on 19 April 1877, the year when Monet exhibited seven versions of *Saint-Lazare Railway Station* at the Third Impressionist Exhibition. After Turner who, in 1844, with *Rain, Steam, Speed*, had chosen the train as a subject, or Daumier with *A Third-Class Carriage* (1864), other artists belonging to the Impressionist generation took up the same theme: Manet, Pissarro, Sisley and Caillebotte. The railway station, with its new glass and metal architecture, symbolised industrial progress and speed: the inauguration of the London Crystal Palace for the World Fair of 1851 had a major influence. In Monet's canvas, the golden light and diffuse curls of bluish smoke blur the engines and metal structures of the brand-new Saint-Lazare Railway Station. The railway station is also the waiting-room for all departures to the fashionable seaside resorts or the suburbs. The painters would not have the monopoly on the railway theme: in 1890, Zola gave Lison, the locomotive in *La Bête humaine*, characteristics reminiscent of humans or animals, and he described railway stations resembling those painted by Monet: "...the glass canopies of the covered halls opened their giant porches, with smoky windows... An express engine, with two large raging wheels, was parked on its own... Swirling, expanding whiteness overflowed from the bridge like a blanket of snow, rising through the iron structures."

Claude Monet,
Train in the Countryside,
circa 1870, oil on canvas, 50 x 65 cm

Claude Monet,
The Railway Bridge at Argenteuil,
circa 1874, oil on canvas, 55 x 72 cm

Henri Fantin-Latour and Édouard Manet

Writers who associated with the painters: Zola, Verlaine, Rimbaud, Mallarmé...

Henri Fantin-Latour,
The Corner of a Table,
1872, oil on canvas, 160 x 225 cm, Salon of 1872

Édouard Manet,
Émile Zola,
1868, oil on canvas, 146.3 x 114 cm

Édouard Manet,
Stéphane Mallarmé,
1876, oil on canvas, 27.5 x 36 cm

Two phenomena are probably behind the very close links between writers and the painters of the "new art". Firstly, since the Salons and Diderot, it had become common knowledge that writers dabbled in painting. This tradition was continued in the 19th century: in 1845, Baudelaire published his first report on the Salon, and this was only the beginning. In 1866, Zola assembled the reviews which he had published in *L'Événement* under the title *Mon Salon*, which he dedicated to Paul Cézanne. From this point of view, the press played a vital role in defending controversial painters: new art journals were created, some of which, such as *L'Artiste*, attracted prestigious writers, namely Champfleury, Baudelaire, Mallarmé, Gautier... A new more novel idea was supported by certain writers, such as Baudelaire, Nerval, Rimbaud and Mallarmé. This was the theory of balance, according to which multiple, mysterious analogies in different domains lay hidden within the depths of the universe: "Nature is a temple in which living pillars / Sometimes allow confused words to escape... / Like long echoes which from afar merge / In deep, dark unity, / As vast as the night and the light, / The perfumes, the colours and the sounds answering each other..." For these poets, painters and writers were able to reach the mysterious unity of the world, the spiritual reality of Beauty. Manet painted a portrait of Zola, who had spoken in his defence in 1866. He also painted the image of the poet Mallarmé in a nonchalant pose, holding a cigar in one hand and flicking through a book: the writer visited the painter in the late afternoon almost every day, for ten years. Lastly, Fantin-Latour portrayed Verlaine and Rimbaud by the side of a few young poets in *The Corner of a Table.*

James Abbott McNeill Whistler and Gustave Caillebotte

All manner of subjects

James Abbott McNeill Whistler,
Arrangement in Grey and Black, No. 1
or *The Artist's Mother,*
1871, oil on canvas, 144.3 x 162.5 cm

"I find it interesting because it is a portrait of my mother; but should the public be concerned with the identity of the model? The merit of the piece should lie in the arrangement." Thus spoke James Whistler (1834-1903) on his *Arrangement in Grey and Black, No. 1* or *The Artist's Mother*, the two titles showing the painter's hesitation between two "subjects". Another *Arrangement in Grey and Black No. 2* or *Thomas Carlyle*, follows exactly the same composition of that at Orsay: the seated figure, painted in profile, stands out from a wall decorated with a few etchings, with an even darker skirting board running along the bottom. Here, the colour forms the composition of the painting and the "orchestra" – it was probably not by chance that, from the end of the 1860s, Whistler often used musical terms for the titles of his paintings, like in this particular instance. The highly diluted colour –

Gustave Caillebotte,
The Planers,
1875, oil on canvas, 102 x 146.5 cm,
2nd Impressionist Exhibition, 1876

greys and blacks –, is almost reminiscent of a wash: “Paint should never be thickly applied. It should be like a breath of air on the surface of a window.” Whistler, initially influenced by Courbet, then attracted by Japanese prints and the Pre-Raphaelites, finally remained unclassifiable. Gustave Caillebotte (1848-1894) was closer to the Impressionists, even though his brushstrokes are smoother than his fellow artists. This is firstly because he was their friend, and then their patron when, after the death of his father, he found himself the owner of a large fortune and, secondly, because his style of painting was rather similar to that of Manet and Degas through his choice of subjects, centring and unusual perspectives, all of which are marvellously illustrated by *The Planers*, which was not at all appreciated by Zola, despite the modern nature of the subject: “Photographing reality, when not enhanced by the original mark of artistic talent, is an appalling thing.”

Gustave Caillebotte,
View over the Roofs (effect of snow)
or *Snow-Covered Roofs,*
1878, oil on canvas, 64 x 82 cm,
4th Impressionist Exhibition, 1879

Comparison of works

The Impressionists and the snow

Charles-François Daubigny,
Snow,
1873, oil on canvas, 90 x 120 cm, Salon of 1873

Claude Monet,
The Cart. Snow-Covered Road in Honfleur,
circa 1867, oil on canvas, 65 x 92.5 cm

Claude Monet,
The Magpie,
1869, oil on canvas,
89 x 130 cm

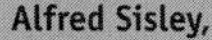

Alfred Sisley,
The Cœur-Volant Coast at Marly in the Snow,
circa 1877-1878, oil on canvas, 46 x 55.5 cm

During the winter when Monet painted *The Cart. Snow-Covered Road in Honfleur*, a journalist from the *Journal du Havre* wrote: "We saw him once. It was in winter, during a few days of snow, when almost all means of communication had been cut off... It was freezing. We first saw a foot-warmer, then an easel, and a man wrapped up in three thick cardigans, with gloved hands, and his face half frozen: it was M. Monet, studying an effect of the snow." He went on to add: "Art has brave soldiers!" Monet and several other Impressionists with him – Sisley and Pissarro – enjoyed painting snow, which constantly changed its appearance with the light and cold air, in cold colours. During the particularly harsh winter of 1879-1880, the Seine was completely frozen, and then melted slowly. "The ice has been cracking terribly here and, naturally, I tried to do something with it", Monet wrote to one of his clients in January 1880. "Everything is sparkling, ... this thaw is turning everything into a mirage: you can no longer tell whether it is the ice or the sun, and all the pieces of ice are shattering and carrying the reflection of the sky, and the trees are so bright that you can no longer tell whether their redness is due to the autumn or their species, and you no longer know where you are, in a river bed or a clearing in the wood." The words of Marcel Proust herald Monet's forthcoming canvases, in which the subject will finally disappear and be replaced by a single subject, the rendering of the changing, transient atmosphere and light. Certain critics would deride these "effects of snow", such as Louis Leroy on the subject of Pissarro's *White Frost* in his famous article in *Charivari*: "Furrows?! Frost?!... Those are marks left by a palette scraped across a soiled canvas. There is no beginning or end, top or bottom, front or back."

Camille Pissarro,
White Frost, The Old Road to Ennery, Pontoise,
1873, oil on canvas, 65 x 93 cm

Camille Pissarro,
Effect of Snow at Éragny,
1894, oil on canvas, 73.5 x 92.5 cm

Claude Monet,
Cracking on the Seine: Blocks of Ice,
circa 1880, oil on canvas, 60 x 100 cm

Alfred Sisley,
Snow at Louveciennes,
1878, oil on canvas, 61 x 50.5 cm

Claude Monet,
Church at Vétheuil, Snow,
1878-1879, oil on canvas, 52 x 71 cm

Berthe Morisot and Mary Cassatt

Two women painters

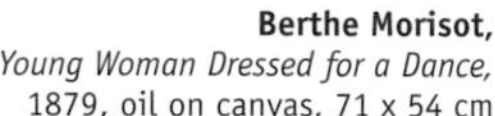

Berthe Morisot,
Young Woman Dressed for a Dance,
1879, oil on canvas, 71 x 54 cm

Mary Cassatt,
Young Girl in the Garden, also known as
Young Girl Working or *Woman Sewing in a Garden,*
circa 1880-1882, oil on canvas, 92 x 63 cm

Perhaps because it was more difficult for a woman in the 19th century to paint musical soirées in cafés or life on the boulevards, Berthe Morisot and Mary Cassatt mainly painted peaceful, intimate scenes of family life in bourgeois interiors and gardens with children playing. "Setting down something that is happening, oh! something, the smallest thing, a smile, a flower, a fruit, the branch of a tree... Such vast ambition." The modest words spoken by Berthe Morisot (1841-1895) with regard to her work must not be misleading. Married to Eugène Manet, brother of Édouard, she spent her whole life among painters, collectors and poets: Renoir, Degas, Monet, Caillebotte, Mallarmé and Valéry. In 1874, during the First Impressionist Exhibition, she was the only woman present, with *The Cradle*, which the organisers hung next to *A Modern Olympia* by Cézanne: "I felt a pang of anguish on seeing your daughter's paintings in this pernicious environment", lamented Guichard, a conventionalist painter who had once taught the young woman, to Berthe Morisot's mother... Another woman, Mary Cassatt (1844-1926), of American origin, who had come to Europe to finish her training, spent almost her entire career in France. Discovered and influenced by Degas, the misogynist – "I cannot believe that a woman is able to draw equally well", she focused solely on the human figure,

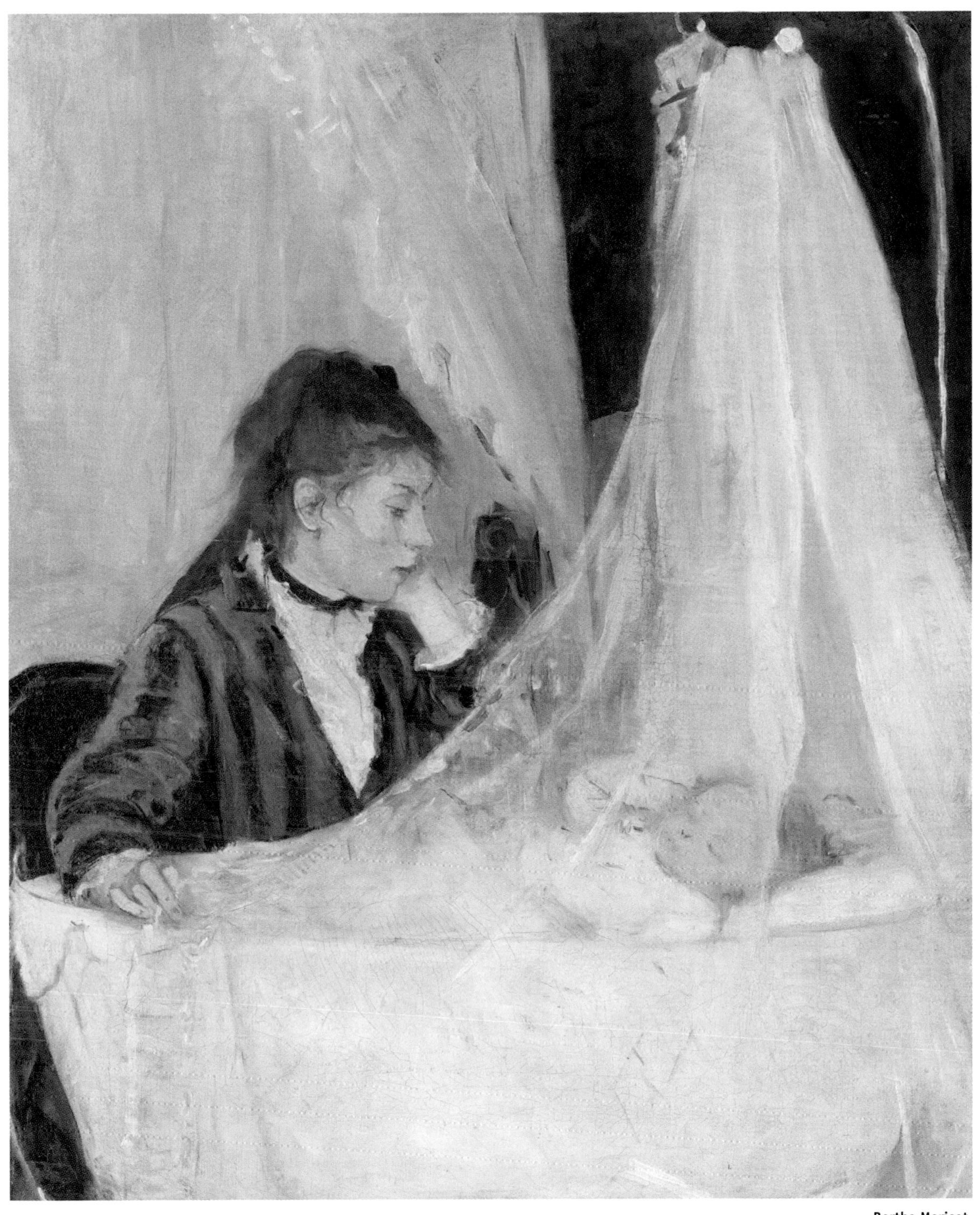

Berthe Morisot,
The Cradle,
1872, oil on canvas, 56 x 46 cm,
1st Impressionist Exhibition, 1874

particularly women and children, which she portrayed in natural poses, both in the open and in the privacy of their homes or at the opera. Like Degas, at the end of her life she produced numerous pastels and etchings. She was also the best living ambassador for Impressionism in the United States, advising museums and collectors – the Palmers, Ryersons and Havemeyers. "It is probably due to the Americans that we have not starved to death", declared Renoir.

Pierre-Auguste Renoir

His Impressionist period, in the 1870s

Pierre-Auguste Renoir,
Woman Reading,
circa 1874, oil on canvas, 46.5 x 38.5 cm

After having started out as a painter on porcelain, Renoir entered to the École des Beaux-Arts and spent some time in Gleyre's studio where he met Bazille, Monet and Sisley. He had a difficult beginning: he had no money, and his few paintings shown at the Salon did not attract much attention. His links with the future Impressionists grew stronger when the great, generous Bazille put him up in his studio and he began more assiduously to keep company with Monet, who had moved to Argenteuil. *Path Leading Through the Tall Grass* perfectly illustrates his Impressionist period, during which he painted landscapes, although it would be the human figure which ultimately dominated his painting. *Woman Reading*, painted with small energetic brushstrokes, foreshadows the painter's subsequent study on the rendering of light in his open-air figures, as seen in *Study. Torso: Effects of Sunlight.* In this piece, exhibited during the Second Impressionist Exhibition, Renoir uses the shadow and light filtering through the almost abstract leaves to bring out the naked torso of his model whose features become blurred under the effect of the light. The critics could not stand this freedom, and in fact reproached the new painters for the unfinished appearance of their work: "Please try therefore", Albert Wolff wrote in *Le Figaro*, "to explain to M. Renoir that the female torso is not a mass of decomposing flesh with green and purple blotches denoting a state of complete putrefaction in a cadaver." Louis Enault, from the *Constitutionnel*, added: "A large study of a nude woman, who, admittedly, ought to have been wearing a dress, grieves us with its purple tones of tainted flesh." Back in 1863, Manet's *Olympia* had already been described as "tainted"!

Pierre-Auguste Renoir,
Path Leading Through the Tall Grass,
circa 1872-1875, oil on canvas, 60 x 74 cm

Pierre-Auguste Renoir,
Study. Torso: Effects of Sunlight,
1875-1876, oil on canvas, 81 x 65 cm,
2nd Impressionist Exhibition, 1876

Edgar Degas

The dance

Edgar Degas,
The Dance Studio at the Opera on Rue Le Peletier,
1872, oil on canvas, 32 x 46 cm

On Friday 13 February 1874, after having visited Degas in his studio for the first time, Edmond de Goncourt wrote in his *Journal*: "Yesterday, I spent the day in the studio of a peculiar painter, named Degas. After numerous attempts, and pushing in every direction, he has become smitten with modern life; and in this modern life, he has set his heart on laundry women and dancers... And, surprised by nature, one is faced with the graceful twisting movements and gestures of these little monkey-girls. The painter shows you his paintings, commenting from time to time on his interpretation by mimicking a choreographic development, by imitating, as expressed by the dancers, one of their arabesques. And it is really very amusing to see him, on tiptoe, with rounded arms, mixing the aesthetics of the painter with that of a ballet master.... An eccentric chap this Degas, sickly, neurotic, with such poor eyesight that he fears losing his sight altogether; but, consequently, an eminently sensitive soul, suffering the consequences of the nature of things. Until now, in copying modern life, this is the man that I have best seen capture the soul of this life." Usually observed from strange angles and situated in the wings or in a rehearsal room, Degas' numerous dancers are all anonymous. The painter does not omit a single detail, be it unexpected or ungraceful. His dancers scratch their backs, yawn, adjust their neck ribbons, and chat... Their nature is simply obvious: "A painting requires as much cunning, malice and vice as in preparing for a crime, simply paint that which is not real and add a natural note."

Edgar Degas,
End of an Arabesque
or *Dancer Curtseying,*
circa 1876-1877,
paint mixed with spirits
touched up with pastel
on canvas, 67 x 38 cm

Edgar Degas, *The Star* or *Dancer on Stage,*
circa 1875-1877, pastel on monotype,
60 x 44 cm, 3rd Impressionist Exhibition, 1877

Edgar Degas, *Group of Dancers,*
1884-1885, pastel, 75 x 73 cm

Edgar Degas,
The Dance Class,
circa 1873-1876, oil on canvas, 85 x 75 cm

Claude Monet

Air, wind, sun and poppies

In a letter to Gimpel dating from 1920, Monet recalled the memory of 30 June 1878, when festivities had been organised during the World Fair to celebrate the rebirth of France: "I loved the flags. On the first national holiday on 30 June, I went for a walk with the tools of my trade, on rue Montorgueil; the road was decked with flags and there were huge crowds; I caught sight of a balcony, I climbed up and asked permission to paint, which I received. Then, I climbed back down incognito! Ah! Those were good times, wonderful times." When he spoke of the "innumerable small black marks at the bottom of the painting" evoking the people walking along the Boulevard des Capucines exhibited during the First Impressionist Exhibition, Louis Leroy had seen nothing yet. In *Rue Montorgueil*, the silhouettes are nothing more than minuscule vertical, shapeless lines in colours matching the blues, whites and reds of the countless flags fastened to the windows of the buildings lining the street: it is up to the onlooker to interpret and reconstruct the strolling crowds and flags flapping in the wind. Faced with a constantly moving reality, the painter no longer seeks to convey the objective reality, since its "true nature" no longer exists, but desires, more modestly, to reproduce his impression of reality. "For an Impressionist, painting from life does not mean painting the object, but to create its feelings", explained Cézanne. It was up to the onlooker to interpret the trail of red marks swaying, stemless, in the long grass, in *Poppies*. Neither Marquet, nor Dufy, would forget Monet's lesson thirty or so years later, when painting the flags flying from the windows at half-mast, on 14 July.

Claude Monet,
Rue Montorgueil. Fête du 30 June 1878,
1878, oil on canvas, 81 x 50.5 cm

Claude Monet,
Poppies, 1873,
oil on canvas, 50 x 65 cm,
1st Impressionist Exhibition, 1874

Claude Monet,
The Luncheon, circa 1873-1874,
oil on canvas, 160 x 201 cm,
2nd Impressionist Exhibition, 1876

Comparison of works

The Impressionists and portraits

Édouard Manet,
Reading,
1865-1875, oil on canvas,
60.5 x 73.5 cm

Édouard Manet,
Berthe Morisot with Bunch of Violets,
1872, oil on canvas, 55 x 38 cm

Édouard Manet,
Stéphane Mallarmé,
1876, oil on canvas, 27.5 x 36 cm

Édouard Manet,
Georges Clemenceau,
1879, oil on canvas, 94.5 x 74 cm

Edgar Degas,
Portraits at the Bourse,
circa 1878-1879,
oil on canvas, 100 x 82 cm

"The flood of portraits grows in size every year and threatens to invade the Salon completely", commented Zola in 1868. This increase was probably related to the desire of the middle-classes to build up a portrait gallery to give their newly acquired fortunes a semblance of nobility. In addition to issues relating to social status, the artists themselves, or at least some of them, needed to make a living from their paintings, and portraits were a godsend – as would be the case for Monet and Renoir. The Impressionist painters were often not content to merely reproduce the physical features and psychology of the model, but rather placed the models in their own world, engaged in their usual occupations, the portrait sometimes becoming a genre scene. This is shown, for example, by the title of Manet's painting, *Reading,* which is nothing more than a portrait of Mme Manet. "With a back", affirmed Duranty, "we want to reveal a temperament, age and social status; with a pair of hands, we must express a magistrate or tradesman; with a gesture, a whole series of emotions". *The Orchestra at the Opera,* in which it is no longer possible to determine whether it is a portrait of bassoonist Désiré Dihau or of all the musicians, perfectly illustrates the painter's aim: "To paint portraits of people in familiar, typical poses, above all to give their face the same range of expression as their body." Renoir probably painted the largest number of commissioned portraits, usually in small sizes of which he was particularly fond: while some of the women in his portraits have been identified, others, such as the *Young Woman with Veil,* whose profile is almost hidden, have retained their anonymity and their secrets.

Edgar Degas,
Mme Jeantaud in the Mirror,
circa 1875, oil on canvas,
70 x 84 cm

Pierre-Auguste Renoir,
Mme Paul Darras, circa 1872-1873,
oil on canvas, 47.5 x 39 cm

Edgar Degas,
The Orchestra at the Opera,
circa 1870, oil on canvas,
56.5 x 46.2 cm

Pierre-Auguste Renoir,
Young Woman with Veil,
1875-1877, oil on canvas, 61 x 51 cm

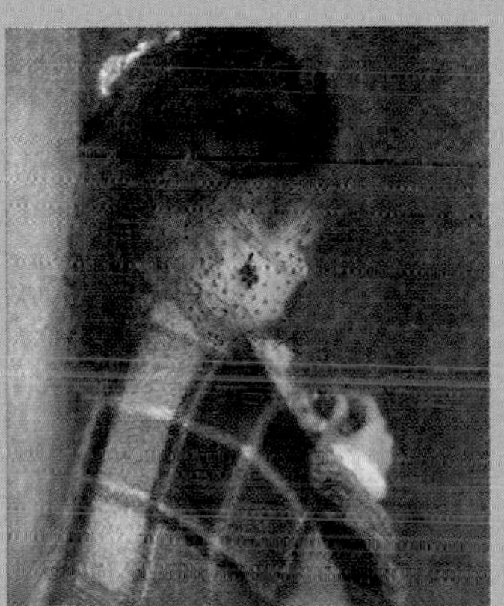

Pierre-Auguste Renoir,
Young Girl Sitting,
1909, oil on canvas,
65.5 x 54.5 cm

Gustave Caillebotte,
Portrait of the Artist,
circa 1889, oil on canvas, 40.5 x 32.5 cm

Pierre-Auguste Renoir,
Mme Georges Charpentier,
1876-1877, oil on canvas, 46.5 x 38 cm,

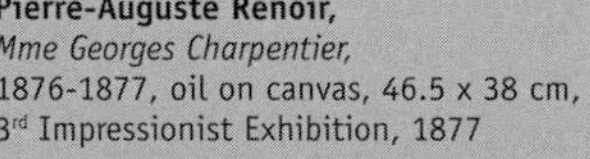

3rd Impressionist Exhibition, 1877

Edgar Degas and Claude Monet

The Impressionists and everyday work

Edgar Degas,
Women Ironing,
circa 1884-1890,
oil on canvas,
76 x 81 cm

By "tackling vast series on people of the world, priests, soldiers, farmers, labourers and merchants", which Duranty recommended to painters, they were able to invent this "new art" where planers, chiropodists, coal heavers and women ironing all found their place. By exhibiting his *Stone Breakers*, which disappeared during the Second World War, at the Salon of 1850-1851, Courbet restored to favour the beauty of working life. "Until now, art has exclusively focused on gods, heroes and saints; it is time that it turned to mere mortals", wrote

Claude Monet,
The Coal Heavers,
1875, oil on canvas, 55 x 66 cm,
2nd Impressionist Exhibition, 1876

Pierre-Joseph Proudhon in 1865. While *The Coal Heavers* seems unusual in Monet's work, which favoured gardens and expanses of water, Degas' Women Ironing returns like a leitmotif: "He places before our eyes, in their poses and limited charms, laundry women, laundry women... speaking their language and technically explaining the pressing method and the circular method, etc.", wrote Edmond de Goncourt in his *Journal*, on 13 February 1874. Degas probably borrowed this theme from Daumier, whom he greatly admired; he also collected his canvases and drawings, together with a great number of lithographs. Degas captured the pose and spontaneous gestures of the figures, as if retranscribing the immediate reality, as was often the case. But one cannot trust appearances. "Never has art been less spontaneous than mine", confessed Degas, "What I do is the result of reflection and studying the great masters. I know nothing of inspiration, spontaneity or temperament..." The number of sketches and numerous canvases on the same theme could persuade one to take his word for it.

Edgar Degas,
The Chiropodist,
1873, paint mixed with spirits
on paper re-mounted on canvas,
61 x 46 cm

Café vogue

Édouard Manet,
Waitress with Beer Glasses,
1879, oil on canvas, 77.5 x 65 cm

It was first at the Café Guerbois, and then at the Café de La Nouvelle-Athènes that artists, and later journalists and critics, regularly met to discuss new ideas. "There was nothing more interesting than these conversations, with the perpetual clash of opinions", explained Monet. "We exercised our minds, we promoted selfless, sincere research... We always came out stronger, with a more steadfast will, thinking more clearly." Manet situated his *Waitress with Beer Glasses* in the Brasserie de Reichshoffen, which provided the décor for many of his paintings during the period. Although Manet continued to show at the official Salon and never took part in an Impressionist exhibition, he was tacitly considered their leader. Even though it was subsequently re-cut, further intensifying the close-up on the two figures, the composition of this piece, influenced by Japanese prints and photography, is related to Degas' work. Objects and figures appear to have been captured at a precise moment: in Manet's piece, the figures are superimposed, the heads overlap each other, certain figures are truncated by the frame; in Degas' piece, the foreground is laid out like a large zigzag punctuated by marble table tops – without legs –, which push the two figures – Marcellin Desboutin, a painter, and Ellen Andrée, an actress – back into the top-right corner. Here, the theme of modern life unites two artists who would compete with each other throughout their lives. This is shown in an anecdote: even though Degas had not made any comments when visiting Manet's studio, he was full of praise when telling a friend what he had seen. Manet was extremely angry that Degas had said nothing to him.

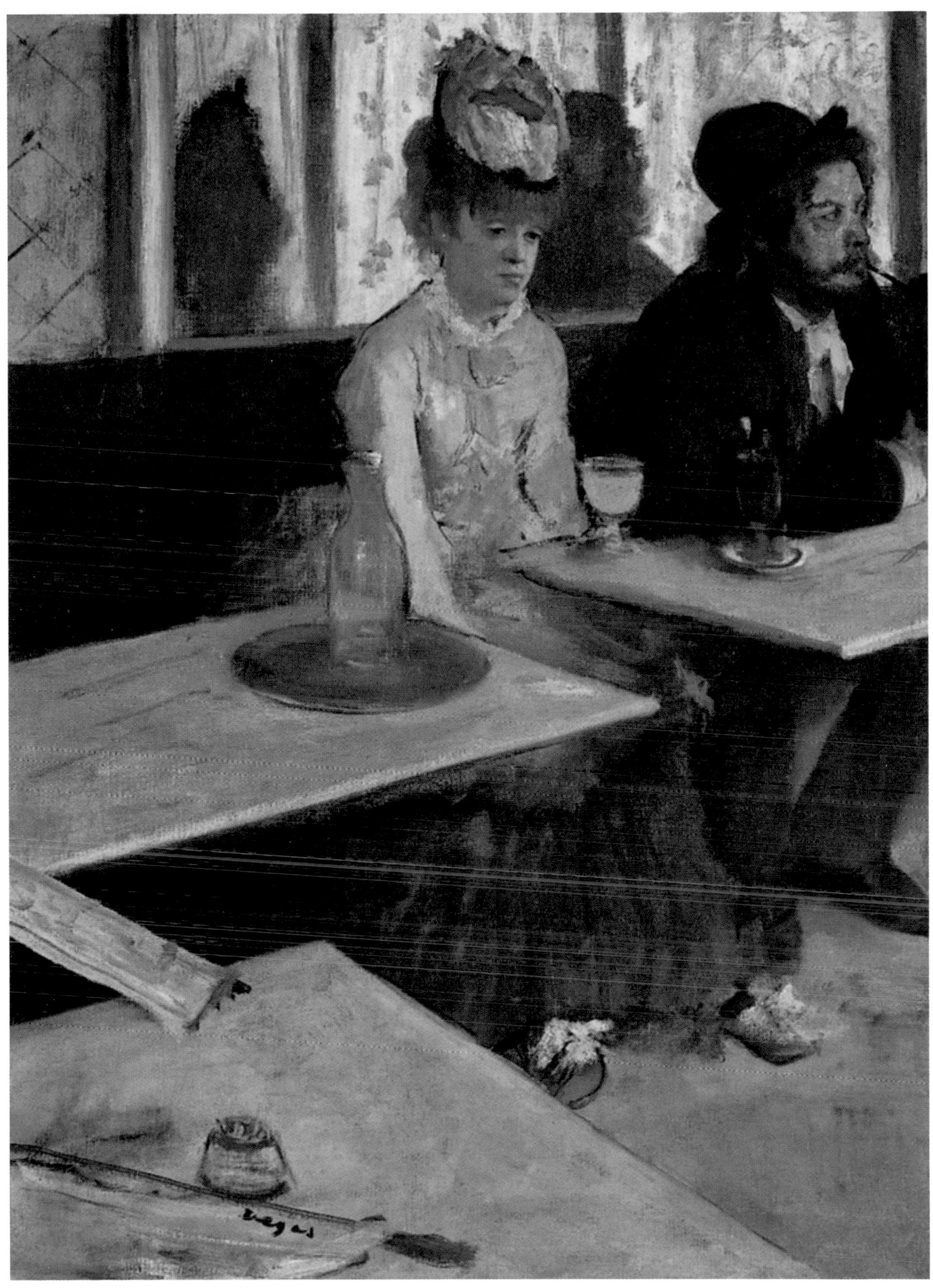

Edgar Degas,
In a Café, also known as *Absinthe,*
1875-1876, oil on canvas, 92 cm x 68 cm

Pierre-Auguste Renoir

Renoir and the 3rd Impressionist Exhibition: 1877

Pierre-Auguste Renoir,
The Swing,
1876, oil on canvas, 92 x 73 cm,
3rd Impressionist Exhibition, 1877

The Swing and *Dancing at the Moulin de la Galette*, painted at the same time in Montmartre and selected for the Third Impressionist Exhibition, were admittedly highly praised, but also incurred the same type of critical remarks as *Study. Torso: Effects of Sunlight*, which had been exhibited the previous year. "The effects of the sun are combined in such a strange way that they produce precisely the effect of greasy marks on the figures' clothes", wrote the critic from *L'Événement* on the subject of *The Swing*. In the two pieces, the light subdued by the foliage falls in coloured patches on the clothes, faces and the ground, vibrating colours which thus tend to dissolve the forms. According to Georges Rivière, a faithful friend of Renoir's, with regard to *Dancing at the Moulin de la Galette*: "We carried this canvas from rue Cortot to the Moulin every day, since the piece was painted entirely on the spot. It was not always straightforward." As for *The Swing*, it may possibly have inspired Zola in *Une page d'amour*, published in 1878: "Standing on the small board, arms outstretched and holding on to the ropes... she wore a grey dress trimmed with mauve ribbons... That day, in the pale sky, golden dust fell from the sun. Slowly raining sun rays between the bare branches." The portrait of Mme Georges Charpentier, which was also shown at the same Impressionist Exhibition, paid tribute to the wife of the publisher of Flaubert, the Goncourt brothers, Daudet and Maupassant. By opening the doors of her salon on rue de Grenelle, where artists, writers and left-wing politicians – Clemenceau and Gambetta – rubbed shoulders, this woman of character allowed the son of a small Parisian tailor to enter bourgeois circles, a world of potential clients.

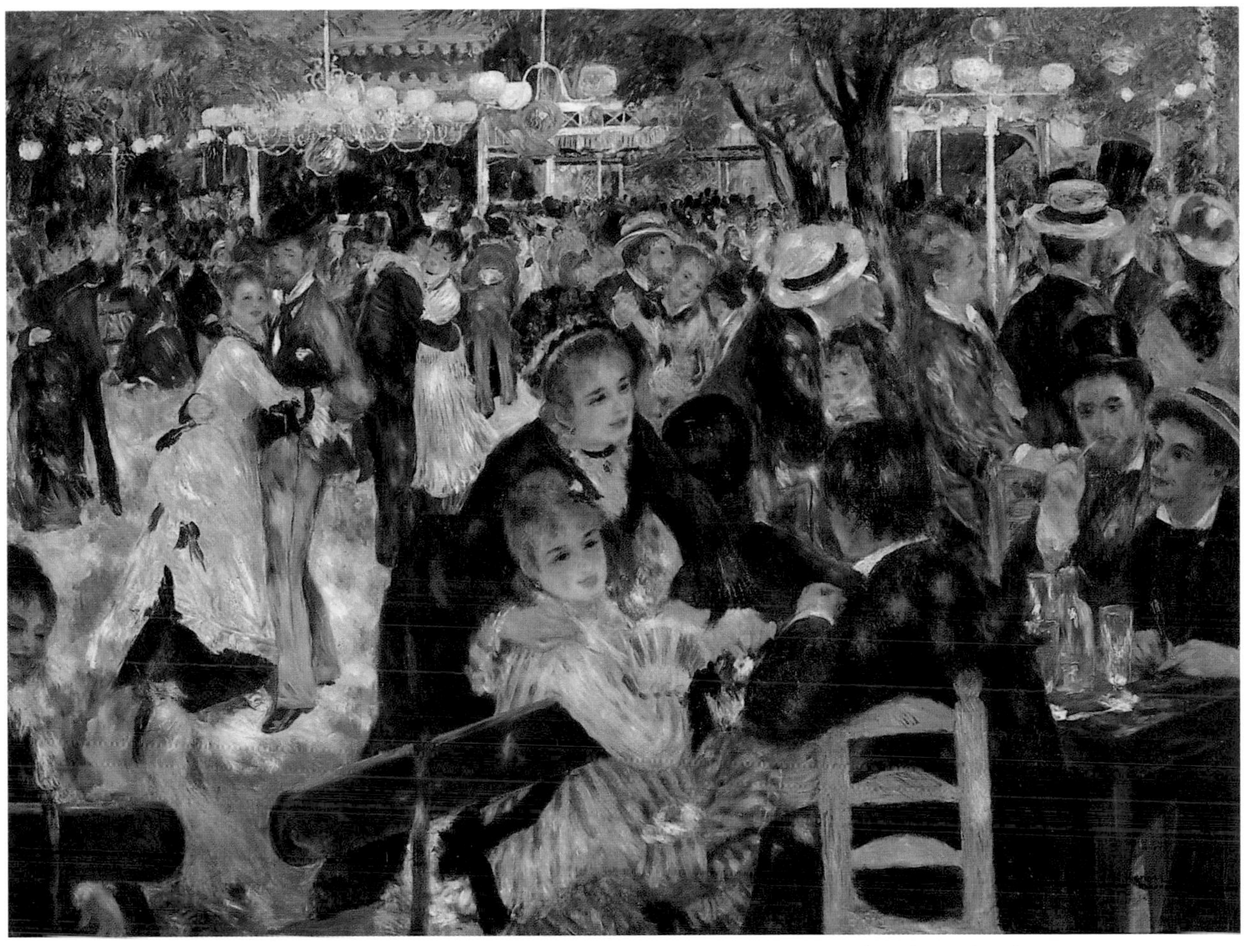

Pierre-Auguste Renoir,
Dancing at the Moulin de la Galette,
1876, oil on canvas, 131 x 175 cm,
3rd Impressionist Exhibition, 1877

Pierre-Auguste Renoir,
Mme Georges Charpentier,
1876-1877, oil on canvas, 46.5 x 38 cm,
3rd Impressionist Exhibition, 1877

Jules Bastien-Lepage, Léon Lhermitte, Constantin Meunier and Fernand Cormon

Naturalist painting during the 3rd Republic

Fernand Cormon,
Cain, after Victor Hugo, *La Légende des siècles*,
1880, oil on canvas, 380 x 700 cm,
Salon of 1880

"He was a realist, who conveyed what he saw, precisely, without passion, without enthusiasm, without spirit; he was not a poet, who interprets nature and life with a thought for the beyond, who embellishes them with his dreams and gives beings and objects tone and form which, in reality, are only reminders of the ideal, the imaginings of visionaries... In *Haymaking*..., intricately developed down to the finest and least visible details, he crushed the figures which faded, became flat and did not appear to belong to the air, trees or sky surrounding them." Octave Mirbeau appreciated neither Jules Bastien-Lepage (1848-1884) nor, more generally, Naturalism which, according to him, was "an absurd, barbaric doctrine". An heir to Realism, Naturalism first served to describe to a certain extent the writings of Zola, Maupassant and Flaubert, who in their novels analysed and described society in the same way that scientists observed nature. The Naturalist painters therefore chose their subjects in rural life, like Bastien-Lepage (*Haymaking*) or Léon Lhermitte (1844-1925), his successor (*Paying the Reapers*), or in working-class urban life, like Constantin Meunier (1831-1905, *In the Black Country*), but unlike the Realist painters they did not combine their art with any controversial intentions as Courbet would do. Furthermore, their palette was lighter, and their brushstrokes generally more flowing, inherited from the Impressionists. Fernand Cormon (1845-1924) took a biblical subject, revisited by Victor Hugo in *La Légende des siècles*, and produced a more naturalist version, devoid of all symbolism: "When with his children clothed in the skins of beasts, / Wild and pallid in the midst of storms, / Cain was cast out from the presence of Jehovah..."

Léon Lhermitte,
Paying the Reapers,
1882, oil on canvas, 215 x 272 cm, Salon of 1882

Constantin Meunier,
In the Black Country,
circa 1893, oil on canvas, 81 x 94.5 cm

Jules Bastien-Lepage,
Haymaking,
1877, oil on canvas,
180 x 195 cm, Salon of 1878

Comparison of works

Intimate moments and childhood

Berthe Morisot,
The Cradle,
1872, oil on canvas,
56 x 46 cm,
1st Impressionist Exhibition, 1874

Pierre-Auguste Renoir,
Julie Manet, known as
Child Holding a Cat,
1887, oil on canvas,
65 x 54 cm

Berthe Morisot,
The Butterfly Hunt, 1874,
oil on canvas, 46 x 56 cm

Mary Cassatt,
Mother and Child,
1897, pastel on cardboard,
55 x 46 cm

Children are often depicted in Impressionist canvases, either their portraits were painted, or they were part of intimate family scenes. This was the case for Berthe Morisot, who mostly portrayed her close family in garden or interior scenes. In *The Cradle* and *The Butterfly Hunt*, she chose to portray her sister, Edma, with her small daughter Blanche. “Mlle Berthe Morisot has some small paintings, with hints of exquisite truthfulness”, wrote Zola in 1876. “I will above all mention two or three highly refined seascapes and landscapes, women and children walking in the long grass.” The theme of mother and child was also one of Mary Cassatt’s favourite themes, which she painted with infinite naturalness, like in the beautiful pastel, *Mother and Child.*

Pierre-Auguste Renoir, Berthe Morisot’s precise contemporary, also painted many children, not only his own, but also those of his friends and patrons: Julie Manet was the daughter of Eugène Manet, the painter’s brother, and Berthe Morisot; *Motherhood* portrays Aline Charigot, whom he would marry a few years later, and their son Pierre: with Jean and Claude, their children, they would often be the subject of his portraits of intimate family scenes. Other compositions, which he would repeat throughout his career, include pretty adolescent middle-class girls engaged in their favourite pastimes without a care in the world: hence, in *Young Girls at the Piano*, a picture of the innocence and charm of youth.

Pierre-Auguste Renoir,
Motherhood, also known as *Child at the Breast*,
1885, oil on canvas, 91.5 x 72 cm

Pierre-Auguste Renoir,
Young Girls at the Piano,
1892, oil on canvas, 116 x 90 cm

Pierre-Auguste Renoir,
Boy with Cat,
1868, oil on canvas, 123 x 66 cm

Pierre-Auguste Renoir,
Fernand Halphen child,
1880, oil on canvas,
46 x 38 cm

Pierre-Auguste Renoir,
Young Girl Wearing
a Straw Hat, circa 1908,
oil on canvas, 46 x 35 cm

Camille Pissarro,
The Shepherdess, also known as *Young Girl with Stick;*
Country Girl Sitting, 1881, oil on canvas,
81 x 64.7 cm

Paul Cézanne

After his Impressionist period, his "Constructivist" period

Paul Cézanne,
The Bridge at Maincy,
circa 1879-1880, oil on canvas, 58.5 x 72.5 cm

"In order to paint a landscape well", Cézanne explained, "I first need to discover the geological foundations. Consider that the history of the world goes back to the day that two atoms collided, when two vortices, two swirling dances of chemicals were combined… Layers were formed, large pieces of the canvas. I mentally sketch out the rocky skeleton." Cézanne would never forget his work in the outdoors alongside Pissarro in Auvers-sur-Oise, at the end of the 1870s, but would attempt to reconcile this experience of the transient with a concern for construction and structure. "I wanted to make Impressionism solid and durable, like the art of the museums", he declared to Maurice Denis at the end of his life. His visits to the South thus became increasingly frequent and longer in duration. There, he painted landscapes in which he split his view into several areas using geometrical forms which were then placed in perspective because, for him, art is "harmony in parallel with nature". "It is necessary to become classical once again through nature, that is through feeling", he continued. In contrast to the Impressionists who used reverberating brushstrokes, Cézanne structured his paintings by applying regular, parallel brushstrokes which create volume, and are described as "modulating". "Relief [le modelé], that is everything, one should not say model [modeler], but modulate [moduler]." In contrast to the Impressionists once again, he is concerned with the durability and stability of things, and not ethereal, hazy atmospheric effects. On the subject of Cézanne's landscapes painted in the South during this period, John Rewald wrote: "His image of the region consists of coloured planes arranged in a firm structure, architecturally irreconcilable with the doctrines of Impressionism."

Paul Cézanne,
L'Estaque, View of the Gulf of Marseille,
circa 1878-1879, oil on canvas, 59.5 x 73 cm

Paul Cézanne,
Poplars,
circa 1879-1882, oil on canvas, 65 x 80 cm

William Bouguereau, Léon Bonnat and Henri Gervex

Official art during the 3rd Republic

Henri Gervex,
Session of the Painting Jury at the Salon des Artistes Français, in a room on the first floor of the Industrial Design Pavilion,
1885, oil on canvas, 299 x 419 cm,
Salon des Artistes Français, 1885

Léon Bonnat,
Jules Grévy,
1879, oil on canvas,
152 x 116 cm, Salon of 1880

With regard to those who continued to take their subjects from Antiquity, Baudelaire, having dipped his pen in acid, wrote: "They have merely transposed common, vulgar life to a Greek setting... We therefore see ancient children playing with an ancient ball and an ancient hoop, ancient dolls and ancient toys!" With his *Birth of Venus*, Bouguereau (1825-1905), the "Cheap Raphael", achieves nothing more. The classical perspective around a central figure, brushstrokes "as perfect as an enamel", as described by the painter himself, everything in his canvas fulfilled the criteria defining the style of the conventionalist painters, those whom Huysmans called "plasterers": "It is no longer even porcelain, it is limp and over-finished!" Are the members of the jury, painted by Henri Gervex (1852-1929), all of whom are recognisable, in the process of judging one such painting in a room on the first floor of the Industrial Design Pavilion, on the Champs-Élysées, before the opening of the Salon? "Every day, the work was prepared by the attendants, an interminable row of paintings placed on the floor, leaning against the picture rail, running through the rooms on the first floor... The judges stood, they hurried through the task as quickly as possible, rejecting the worst canvases without voting; nevertheless, arguments would sometimes hold up the group, they would quarrel for ten minutes...", related Zola in *L'Œuvre*, in 1886. One could almost be there! Showered with honours and also flattered by the official reviews, Léon Bonnat (1833-1922), a great collector, supporter of Manet and a friend of Degas', who had also taught Toulouse-Lautrec and Dufy, established his reputation, reaching as far as the United States, on the basis of his portraits of key figures of the Third Republic. It has to be said that the man had a sound technique: his portraits, almost photographic, are perfectly finished.

William Bouguereau,
The Birth of Venus,
1879, oil on canvas,
300 x 216 cm, Salon of 1879

Édouard Manet

The "Saint Francis of the still-life"

At the end of his life, Manet regularly sent his close friends small still-lives or letters accompanied by watercolours and poems, in which humour contended with delicacy. A client, Charles Ephrussi, who had paid him more than the requested price for an initial still-life, *A Bunch of Asparagus*, was surprised to receive a second, entitled *Asparagus*, accompanied by this delightful note: "There was one missing from your bunch." In these small still-lives, Manet arranged only a few pieces of fruit, and occasionally just one as in *Lemon*. "A painter can express any thing with fruit, flowers or clouds alone... I would like to be the Saint Francis of the still-life", he confided in the dealer Vollard. In his final years, and in very poor health, he painted numerous simple bouquets of flowers, "not 'manufactured' ones, but others, the true ones", as he would say. Flowers and greenery were arranged naturally in transparent vases which revealed the entangled stems: a few delicate pink Chinese carnations, a purplish-blue clematis... One of the lucky recipients of his bouquets wrote to him on 3 November 1882: "I love the flowers, particularly the white lilies and the roses. By sending me something that will never fade, you have given me the most delightful pleasure. I am proud to think that a great artist took up his brushes and started working again for me... What enchants me even more, is that this beautiful bouquet must be a clear sign for the Manet ladies that the health of someone on whom they lavished such tender care has now returned." Manet died a few months later.

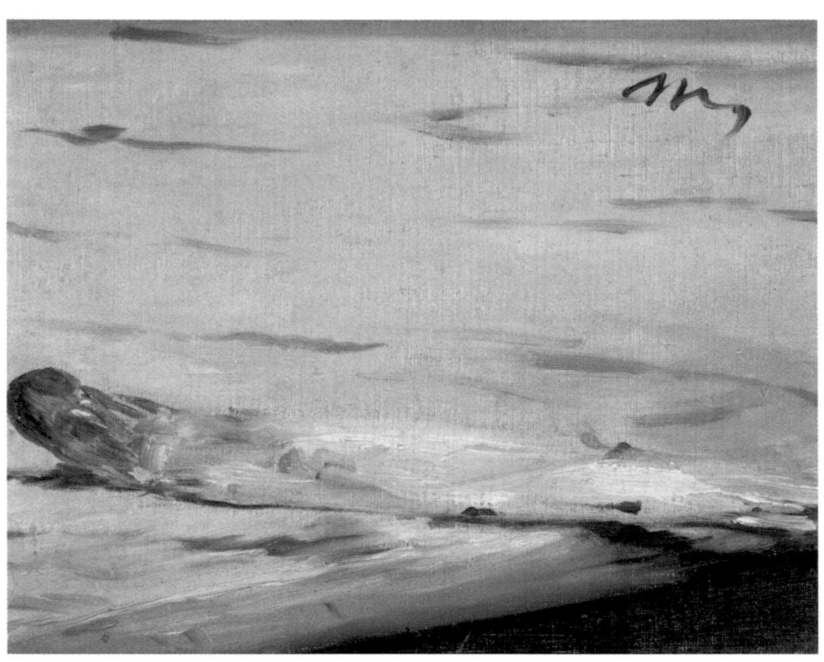

Édouard Manet,
Asparagus, 1880,
oil on canvas, 16.5 x 21.5 cm

Édouard Manet,
Lemon, 1880-1881,
oil on canvas, 14 x 21 cm

Édouard Manet,
Carnations and Clematis in a Crystal Vase,
circa 1882,
oil on canvas,
56 x 35 cm

Paul Cézanne

The still-life

Paul Cézanne,
Apples and Oranges,
circa 1895-1900, oil on canvas,
74 x 93 cm

"I want to amaze Paris with an apple", announced Cézanne. *In The Art of Spiritual Harmony*, Kandinsky wrote: "He turned a cup of tea into a being with a soul or, more precisely, he perceived life in this cup. He has raised the "still-life" to the rank of an externally "dead" but internally living object. He has handled the objects in the same way he handles man, because he has the gift of being able to discover inner life in everything. He takes them and gives them over to colour. They are given life – inner life – and an essentially pictorial essence. He imposes upon them a form that can be reduced to abstract, often mathematical formulae, from which emanates a radiant harmony. He wants to represent neither man nor apple nor tree; Cézanne uses this to create a painting which conveys an inner tone which is called the image." For Cézanne, who painted some two hundred still-lives, objects lend themselves better than figures to in-depth analysis: "I paint still-lives", he said to Renoir. "Female models frighten me. The strumpets are always watching you to catch you when you are off-guard. You always have to be on the defensive, and the subject disappears." From the 1890s, the composition of his still-lives, often viewed from above, became increasingly intricate and continued more and more to evade classical perspective and the illusion of depth. He indefinitely arranged the objects at different angles which had nothing to do with chance – it is said that he placed coins or pieces of wood under certain objects to tilt them and display them as he saw fit. Certain fruits or objects are portrayed from several viewpoints, which would be repeated by the Fauves and the Cubists – a certain form of Cubism would even be described as "Cézanne's cubism", and Matisse declared: "He was our master."

Paul Cézanne, *Green Apples,*
circa 1872-1873, oil on canvas,
26 x 32 cm

Paul Cézanne,
Still-Life with Onions,
circa 1895, oil on canvas, 66 x 82 cm

Paul Cézanne, *The Blue Vase,*
circa 1885-1887, oil on canvas,
61 x 50 cm

Pierre Puvis de Chavannes and Eugène Carrière

The first Symbolists

Pierre Puvis de Chavannes,
The Poor Fisherman,
1881, oil on canvas, 155.5 x 192.5 cm

The term "Symbolists" describes writers or painters whose work is characterised, to a greater or lesser extent, by ambiguity, dreams, the imagination, hermetism or the absence of a subject, a certain mistrust for analysis, and the idea that art and literature have given birth to worlds outside of reality. Puvis de Chavannes (1824-1898) was one such painter, whose name is still linked to major public commissions and whose art appears rather academic. However, at the end of the 19th century, his work, which was considered highly innovative, was regularly slated by the critics and rejected by the Salon, while he was admired by numerous painters, sometimes far removed from the Symbolists: Seurat, Van Gogh, Gauguin, Redon, Maurice Denis, the other Nabis, Hodler, Picasso and Matisse. Moreover, for his 70th birthday, writers and painters organised a huge banquet bringing together a number of artists including Gauguin, Monet, Signac, Zola, Bourdelle and Renoir, and during which tributes by

Pierre Puvis de Chavannes,
Young Girls by the Sea,
1879, oil on canvas, 205 x 154 cm,
Salon of 1879

Eugène Carrière,
Paul Verlaine,
1890, oil on canvas,
61 x 51 cm

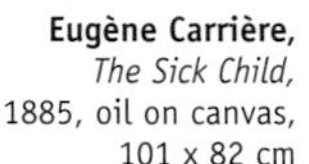

Eugène Carrière,
The Sick Child,
1885, oil on canvas,
101 x 82 cm

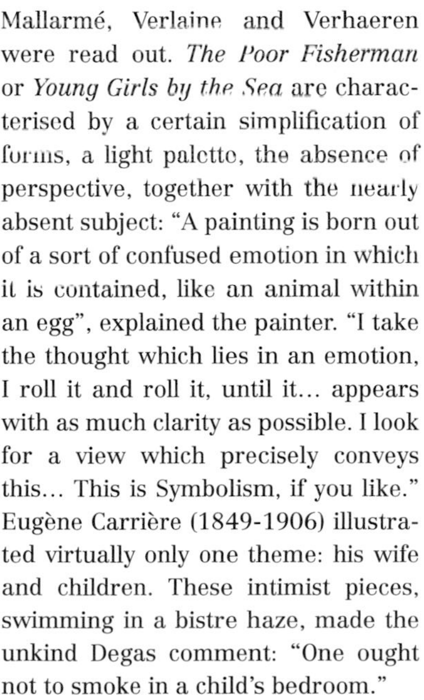

Mallarmé, Verlaine and Verhaeren were read out. *The Poor Fisherman* or *Young Girls by the Sea* are characterised by a certain simplification of forms, a light palette, the absence of perspective, together with the nearly absent subject: "A painting is born out of a sort of confused emotion in which it is contained, like an animal within an egg", explained the painter. "I take the thought which lies in an emotion, I roll it and roll it, until it... appears with as much clarity as possible. I look for a view which precisely conveys this... This is Symbolism, if you like." Eugène Carrière (1849-1906) illustrated virtually only one theme: his wife and children. These intimist pieces, swimming in a bistre haze, made the unkind Degas comment: "One ought not to smoke in a child's bedroom."

Dancing: in the town, in the countryside

On 21 November 1881, Renoir, having left for Italy, wrote to Durand-Ruel: "I went to see the Raphaels in Rome, they are truly beautiful and something I should have seen sooner. They are full of knowledge and wisdom. He did not seek after the impossible, like me. But they are beautiful. I prefer Ingres in oil paintings. But the frescoes, their simplicity and size are admirable." Thus began Renoir's "Ingresque" period which includes *Dancing in the Town* and *Dancing in the Countryside*: the composition has been simplified, the contours of the figures are more distinct and clearer, even though colour is still used with great freedom to model the forms within the contours. "Towards 1883, there was a kind of rupture in my work. I had got to the end of Impressionism and I realised that I could neither paint nor draw. In a word, I had reached a dead end," Renoir confided in Ambroise Vollard. Towards the beginning of the 1880s, Degas' theories, which some of his fellow painters had, until then, found reactionary, began to be brought back into favour by several Impressionists: they questioned the consequences of the way in which the Impressionists handled the light which ultimately dissolved the forms. Concepts such as the primacy of drawing, the absence of spontaneity, the example of the old masters and working in the studio were thus reintroduced by certain artists. During the 1880s, Pissarro wrote to his son, also a painter, and urged him on several occasions to "dedicate more time to drawing and to draw more often – think of Degas". In Renoir's paintings on the theme of *Bathers* dating from this period, he uses an almost smooth, enamel-like technique. However, he would gradually return to a colour and brush-stroke entirely free from constraints which he would never abandon again.

Pierre-Auguste Renoir,
Dancing in the Town,
1883, oil on canvas, 180 x 90 cm

Pierre-Auguste Renoir,
Dancing in the Countryside,
1883, oil on canvas, 180 x 90 cm

Claude Monet

"Painting the land and the air"

Claude Monet, *Study of a figure in the open air,* known as *Woman Holding an Umbrella, turning towards the left* 1886, oil on canvas, 131 x 88 cm

On 13 August 1887, Monet announced to Duret: "I am working like never before, and making new attempts, on figures in the open air as I understand them, painted like landscapes. It is an old dream which still plagues me and that I would like once to achieve; but it is so difficult! In short, I am taking great trouble, it is absorbing me to the point of almost making me ill..." Although, at the start of his career, the painter had attempted to include large figures in a landscape (*The Picnic, Women in the Garden*), he gave up the challenge, which he then took up again in 1885. His aim was not to paint the portrait of Suzanne Hoschedé, the daughter of his second wife, whose features he barely sketched, but he was rather concerned here, like in the series of *Haystacks* a few years later, with painting the air and light at a given moment. "The light in these few canvases speaks the same language as the light in the landscape of the haystacks," explained Gustave Geffroy... "Whether he spreads before our eyes a meadow with red flowers... or raises willowy, rhythmical, sylphlike figures of young women, in the golden sun and passing clouds, he will always be the incomparable painter of the earth and air, preoccupied with the fleeting effects of light on the depths of the universe. He conveys the feeling of the transient moment, which has just been born, which dies, and which will never return... He reveals the changing portraits, the faces of the landscapes, the appearance of joy and despair, mystery and inevitability, with which we adorn all that surrounds us, in our image."

Claude Monet, *Study of a figure in the open air,* known as *Woman Holding an Umbrella, turning towards the right,* 1886, oil on canvas, 131 x 88 cm

Claude Monet, *Haystacks, end of the summer,* 1891, oil on canvas, 60.5 x 100.5 cm

Comparison of works

Cafés, dances and races, or Parisian life

Edgar Degas,
The Racetrack, Amateur Jockeys near a Carriage,
begun in 1876, completed in 1887,
oil on canvas, 66 x 81 cm

Edgar Degas,
Women on the Terrace of a Café, in the Evening,
1877, pastel on monotype,
54.5 x 71.5 cm,
3rd Impressionist Exhibition, 1877

Henri de Toulouse-Lautrec,
The Female Clown, Cha-U-Kao,
1895, oil on cardboard, 64 x 49 cm

Musical soirées in cafés were one of the most fashionable pastimes in Paris during the Second Empire and the Third Republic: at the beginning of the 1880s, there were more than two hundred cafés providing musical entertainment at the bottom of the Butte Montmartre or on the boulevards. These were known as *Les Ambassadeurs, La Cigale, L'Eldorado, Les Folies-Bergère* or *Le Moulin-Rouge*, the future birthplace of the French cancan. In an occasionally shady atmosphere, girls would rub shoulders with elegant gentleman yearning for adventure, as well as acrobats, conjurers, clowns, chansonniers and singers. Cafés, dances, musical soirées and races are recurring themes in the work of Manet, Renoir, and perhaps especially Degas and Toulouse-Lautrec, the former illustrating them sometimes with pastels and the latter using oil on cardboard. "Once," recounted John Rewald, "after a merry evening, Lautrec took a group of friends at dawn to visit a collector, Mlle Dihau, who welcomed them with some hesitation into her modest apartment. Lautrec then led his companions to Degas' canvases and ordered them to kneel in front of them, as a tribute to the revered master." In the work of both artists, the pale, ghostly figures, caught in flight, come out of the frame in the glare of the gas footlights which, coming from below, emphasises the facial features and movements, turning them into a caricature. The artificial light demanded the full interest of the two artists, to the detriment of natural light which attracted most of the Impressionists.

Edgar Degas,
In a Café, also known as *Absinthe*,
1875-1876, oil on canvas,
92 x 68 cm

Henri de Toulouse-Lautrec,
Dancing at the Moulin-Rouge or *La Goulue and Valentin le Désossé*,
1895, oil on canvas, 298 x 316 cm,
panel for La Goulue's booth, at the Foire du Trône in Paris

Henri de Toulouse-Lautrec,
The Moorish Dance or *The Egyptian Dancing Girls*,
1895, oil on canvas, 285 x 307.5 cm,
panel for La Goulue's booth,
at the Foire du Trône in Paris

Édouard Manet,
Waitress with Beer Glasses,
1878-1879, oil on canvas,
77.5 x 65 cm

Edgar Degas,
Musical Soirée at Les Ambassadeurs,
1885, pastel,
26.5 x 29.5 cm

Henri de Toulouse-Lautrec,
Jane Avril Dancing,
circa 1892, oil on cardboard,
85.5 x 45 cm

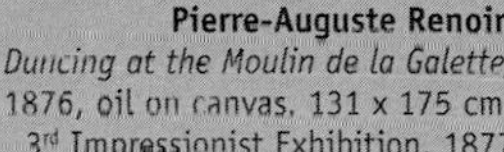

Pierre-Auguste Renoir,
Dancing at the Moulin de la Galette,
1876, oil on canvas, 131 x 175 cm,
3rd Impressionist Exhibition, 1877

Camille Pissarro

Reflections of the "Patriarch" of Impressionism

Camille Pissarro,
Country Girl Making a Fire. White Frost, 1887-1888,
oil on canvas, 92,8 x 92,5 cm,
Brussels, The XX, 1889

Pissarro's long life (1830-1903) allowed him to develop his painting. During the first twenty-five years of his life, he mainly painted landscapes. However, from the 1880s, probably influenced by Degas and his portraits of Parisian factory girls, he became increasingly interested in the human figure, even though he was less concerned with precisely describing the movements and poses related to certain tasks and despite the fact that he focused mainly on the world of countrywomen. Close up, his women simply attend to banal chores, when not idle. Like most of the Impressionists in the 1880s, Pissarro felt the need to find solutions for the fading forms and destructured compositions which had resulted from Impressionism. His interest in the human figure, in sound compositions in which the landscape no longer served as a backdrop and became almost abstract, was one of the solutions for the disappearing subject. Towards 1885-1886, another development, this time stylistic, characterised his work since he was then using the pointillist technique of the Neo-Impressionists, Seurat and Signac, whom he met in 1885. Using small juxtaposed brushmarks in pure colours, Pissarro exhibited alongside them during the eighth and final Impressionist Exhibition in 1886. However, he rapidly discovered the limitations of this technique: "It is so slow," he complained to his dealer, "it takes me three or four times as long to finish a canvas!" In 1889, he rejected the method in order to adopt a more flowing brushmark, painting landscapes once again, according to where his journeys took him.

Camille Pissarro,
Woman in a Field, Spring Sun in the Meadow at Éragny,
1887, oil on canvas, 54.5 x 65 cm

Camille Pissarro,
The Shepherdess, also known as *Young Girl with Stick; Country Girl Sitting*, 1881, oil on canvas, 81 x 64.7 cm

Vincent Van Gogh

The revelation in Paris, 1886

Vincent van Gogh,
Portrait of the Artist,
autumn 1887, oil on canvas, 44.1 x 35.1 cm

Vincent van Gogh,
Dance Hall in Montmartre,
1886, oil on canvas,
49.5 x 64.5 cm

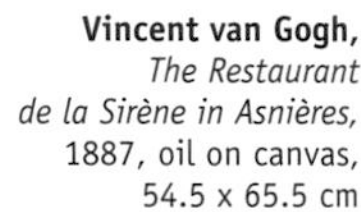

Vincent van Gogh,
The Restaurant de la Sirène in Asnières,
1887, oil on canvas,
54.5 x 65.5 cm

It was only at the age of twenty-seven that Van Gogh (1853-1890) finally chose to become a painter, abandoning his plans to become a minister like his father: "I said to myself: I will pick up my pencil, I will start to draw again, and since then everything has changed for me." When he arrived in Paris in 1886 to join his brother Theo, his painting was still dark and impasted, and his subjects taken from the harsh life of workers in his country. He nevertheless discovered colour in Antwerp at the Rubens Museum and by collecting Japanese prints, but knew nothing of life in Paris. He settled in Montmartre and joined Cormon's studio, where he met Émile Bernard and Toulouse-Lautrec, discovered the Impressionists, and also Seurat, Gauguin and Signac. He learned with astonishing speed. While *Dance Hall in Montmartre* still corresponded to his Dutch style, *The Italian Woman* demonstrates the development in his painting. Manet's former model ran a café in Montmartre, *Le Tambourin*, frequented by Van Gogh, where he exhibited his paintings and Japanese prints. She stands out on a yellow background, without shade or depth: one cannot tell whether she is placing her hands on her lap or on a slightly tilted pedestal table. The randomly coloured stripes are applied with energetic brushstrokes. Like Renoir a few years previously in *Study. Torso: Effects of Sunlight*, he dared to undermine the sacrosanct portrayal of the human figure, using green for the face. In the idea of the "beautiful painting", the body and face are elements which should be left alone. Van Gogh thus led the way for the Fauves, followed by the German Expressionists who would also break this taboo: a painting by Matisse entitled *Portrait of Mme Matisse with Green Stripe* would create a scandal, with others, in 1905.

Vincent van Gogh,
The Italian Woman, alias Agostina Segatori,
end of 1887, oil on canvas, 81 x 60 cm

Georges Seurat

Sketches at the origin of Neo-Impressionism

Georges Seurat,
Study for "A Sunday Afternoon at the Island of La Grande Jatte",
1884, oil on wood, 15.5 x 25 cm

The Impressionist Exhibition of 1886, the last one, rather marked the decline in the movement. Renoir, who had distanced himself from the Impressionists at the beginning of the 1880s, did not take part in the exhibition, together with Monet and Sisley, whose work was, however, continuing along the same lines, while other artists, far removed from the Impressionists, were exhibiting. This was the case for Georges Seurat (1859-1891) who, with a large composition, *A Sunday Afternoon at the Island of La Grande Jatte* (Art Institute, Chicago), also proposed a remedy for the disappearing forms resulting from Impressionism. The rigidity of the figures and the divided brushstrokes, far from shattering volume, gave it density and resonance. Abandoning the broad, spontaneous brushmarks with the mixed colours of the "romantic" Impressionists, he used evenly juxtaposed small dots of pure colour, restricting his palette to three colours: red, yellow, blue – sometimes green. The chemical mixing of colours on the palette was thus replaced by the optical mixing taking place in the retina of the onlooker, giving the painting greater colour intensity and more light. This "young man obsessed with drawing" wanted to give Impressionism scientific rigour. In order to produce his large compositions, he painted "croquetons", or sketches, which were still linked to Impressionism through the themes, working from life, the light palette and the disorderly brushmarks. However, the hieratic nature of the figures, the geometry of the composition and the format of the final pieces reflect a certain classicism. Paradoxically, his "pointillist" technique never led him to renounce his fondness for line: this is revealed in the small sketches for *Models*, in which the line is ultimately suggested by colour.

Georges Seurat,
Study for "Bathing at Asnières",
1883, oil on wood, 15.5 x 25 cm

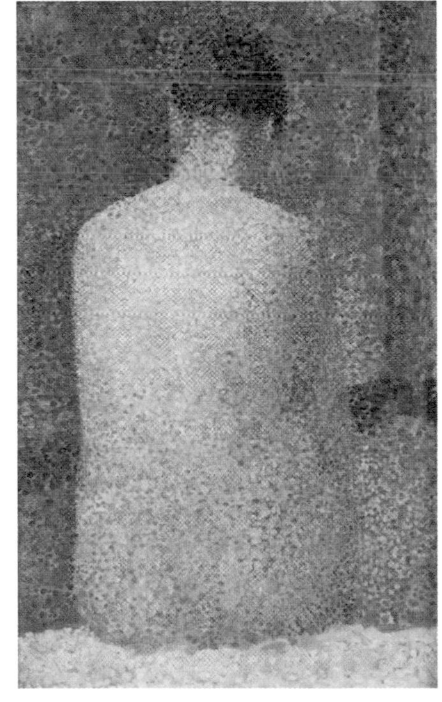

Georges Seurat,
Model From Behind, circa 1886-1887,
study for Models,
oil on wood, 24.5 x 15.5 cm

Georges Seurat and Paul Signac

The untimely death of "the apostle of painting with small dots"

Every or nearly every summer, the "apostle of painting with small dots", as he was nicknamed by Arsène Alexandre, would settle on the coast of the Channel: using his drawings and sketches, in his studio Seurat painted stable, rigid, emotionally restrained landscapes, – which some would call inexpressive – using increasingly round and regular brushmarks, as seen in *Port-en-Bessin, Outer Harbour (High Tide)*. The same quietness is no longer present in *The Circus*, an unfinished canvas arranged according to diagonals and curves on a regular geometrical background made up of horizontals and verticals. "M. Seurat is well aware that a line, regardless of its topographical role, possesses an assessable abstract value", wrote the critic Fénéon, a great supporter of Neo-Impressionism, who thus took up Charles Henry's theory according to which the direction of the lines in a painting either has an "inhibitory", i.e. depressing function, or a "dynamogenic", i.e. exhilarating function. During the same period, Van Gogh and Gauguin attempted to define the psychological impact of colour. When his *Circus* was being hung at the Salon des Indépendants of 1891, Seurat caught a chill and died a few days later: he had not even turned thirty-two. His early death made Signac the leader of the movement. The two painters had met in 1884, during the first Salon des Indépendants. Signac, a self-taught artist fascinated by Monet, was still painting Impressionist landscapes. However, this encounter had a decisive effect: Signac soon began to use optical mixtures and "pointillist" brushmarks, described as such by his disparagers, the hard-line Impressionists, but also a new artist on the scene, Gauguin, who described Seurat and Signac as "little young chemists who accumulate little dots".

Paul Signac,
Les Andelys. The Bank,
1886, oil on canvas, 65 x 81 cm

Georges Seurat,
Port-en-Bessin, Outer Harbour (High Tide),
1888, oil on canvas, 67 x 82 cm, Brussels, The XX, 1889

Georges Seurat,
The Circus,
1890-1891, oil on canvas,
185.5 x 152.5 cm,
Salon des Indépendants, 1891

Vincent Van Gogh

In Arles, from February 1888

Vincent van Gogh,
Starry Night,
1888, oil on canvas, 72.5 x 92 cm

After eighteen months in Paris, Van Gogh found himself in poor health: even though he painted prolifically, his anguish returned and he fell out with everyone: "And then I withdrew to a place in the South, so as not to see so many painters who disgust me as people." Why did he choose Arles? No-one can say. He arrived there on 20 February 1888. Thus began a period in which discouragement and enthusiasm alternated, while the art of this man from the North opened up to the new light of the South. Although his financial situation remained precarious – he sold nothing, went through a number of crises and emerged exhausted –, he painted like a maniac: in little over a year, he produced more than a hundred drawings and watercolours, and close on two hundred paintings the style of which finally broke free from Impressionist and Divisionist influences. His contours are sharp, his line incisive, and he boldly juxtaposes pure colours. He went even further. On 11 August, he wrote the following on the subject of the portrait of *Eugène Bloch, Belgian Painter*, on

Vincent van Gogh,
Eugène Boch, Belgian Painter, September 1888, oil on canvas, 60 x 45 cm

Vincent van Gogh,
The Woman of Arles (Mme Ginoux),
November 1888, oil on canvas,
92.5 x 73.5 cm

which he was working: "To finish [the painting] I will now become a random colourist. I exaggerate the blond hair, I arrive at orange-coloured tones, chromes, pale lemon. Behind the head, instead of painting the banal wall of the shabby apartment, I paint infinity, I paint a simple background of the richest, most intense blue that I can make, and through this simple combination, the blond head, lit up on this rich blue background, creates a mysterious effect like a star in the deep skies." He would henceforth choose colours according to the feelings that they induce. "Instead of attempting to convey that which is before my eyes, I use colour more randomly to express myself strongly", he wrote in 1888. His influence on Fauvism and Expressionism is well known.

Gauguin and Van Gogh in Arles

Vincent van Gogh,
The Dance Hall at Arles,
1888, oil on canvas, 65 x 81 cm

Gauguin complained of his lack of money in his letters to Vincent, hence Theo, a picture dealer, had the idea of bringing him to Arles, where he would support him in exchange for one painting a month. Rather reserved initially, Vincent became more and more enthusiastic: the solitude was getting him down, and he eventually dreamed of a house where several painters would work together and inspire each other. He thus decided to rent the "yellow house", which he fitted out in anticipation of Gauguin's arrival. The latter finally arrived in Arles on 23 October 1888. The two painters worked on the same subjects – Mme Ginoux (The Woman of Arles), Mme Roulin, the Sunflowers, the Washerwomen, the Alyscamps, their portraits –, usually with Gauguin taking up a subject that had already been painted by Van Gogh. Although Gaugin would have preferred a more one-sided influence, both men learned from each other, no matter what he said. In *The Dance Hall at Arles*, the flat colours, simplified forms and black outlines around the contours were inspired by Gauguin who persuaded him to paint "from memory" based on the emotions kindled by the things and the people. As for Gauguin, his vivid and occasionally random colours – the blue trunk and red spot of the bush in *The Alyscamps* – reveal Van Gogh's influence. However, the two artists, who seemed so close in their letters, were of very different dispositions, and tension began to mount. On 23 December, in a rage, Van Gogh threatened Gauguin with an open razor and then cut off his own ear. He was admitted to the general hospital the following day: during the day, he would paint outside and in the yellow house, and in the evening he would return. The neighbours became worried and soon the painter no longer left the hospital. At the beginning of May, he asked to be admitted to an asylum near Saint-Rémy-de-Provence as an "inmate". He wrote to his brother, to whom he sent his canvases: "There are a whole load of daubs inside... Now, as for me, I will never mean anything as a painter, of that I am certain."

Vincent van Gogh,
The Woman of Arles (Mme Ginoux),
November 1888, oil on canvas,
92.5 x 73.5 cm

which he was working: "To finish [the painting] I will now become a random colourist. I exaggerate the blond hair, I arrive at orange-coloured tones, chromes, pale lemon. Behind the head, instead of painting the banal wall of the shabby apartment, I paint infinity, I paint a simple background of the richest, most intense blue that I can make, and through this simple combination, the blond head, lit up on this rich blue background, creates a mysterious effect like a star in the deep skies." He would henceforth choose colours according to the feelings that they induce. "Instead of attempting to convey that which is before my eyes, I use colour more randomly to express myself strongly", he wrote in 1888. His influence on Fauvism and Expressionism is well known.

Paul Gauguin

First an amateur painter

Paul Gauguin,
The Seine at the Pont d'Iéna,
1875, oil on canvas, 65 x 92 cm

Gauguin (1848-1903) was still only an amateur painter when he met Pissarro: "He was one of my masters and I do not deny it." Until then he had only painted canvases with Impressionist brushstrokes: his landscapes, such as *The Seine at the Pont d'Iéna*, are totally in keeping with those by Pissarro or Sisley, while his intimate scenes or still-lives make use of Degas' bold centring – the latter being his constant support. He nevertheless remained an amateur painter since he worked as a stockbroker, which enabled him to build up a fine collection: Impressionist paintings and, in particular nine Pissarros, and five Cézannes which he "treasured" – the latter would influence him the most by far. With the stockmarket collapse in 1882, Gauguin, married with five children, was made redundant: at the age of thirty-four, he thus became a professional painter and moved to Rouen, hoping to earn a living more easily by painting. However, his hopes were rapidly shattered, and his wife decided to move back to Denmark with their children, where he finally joined them. This visit was a disaster and Gauguin soon returned to Paris with his eldest son. The winter of 1885 was very harsh. In July 1886, he gathered enough money to move to Pont-Aven. For many artists, Brittany then represented a return to the simple life. One could discover "the human being in his native freedom, as created on the first day of the world", according to the writings of Flaubert and Maxime du Camp in *Un voyage en Bretagne*. The forests were mysterious, the ordeals primitive, the moors and coasts lonely, and the customs handed down by the generations. Gauguin lived at the Gloanec boarding house, where inexpensive board and lodging could be paid for on credit. He discovered an artists colony there. However, he was disappointed by his stay. He returned to Paris and decided to leave for Panama, followed by Martinique, but returned shortly after, in poor health. He had still not managed to find his way.

Paul Gauguin,
Washerwomen at Pont-Aven,
1886, oil on canvas, 71 x 90 cm

Paul Gauguin,
Still-Life with Mandolin,
1885, oil on canvas, 61 x 51 cm

Émile Bernard

A decisive encounter for Gauguin, summer 1888

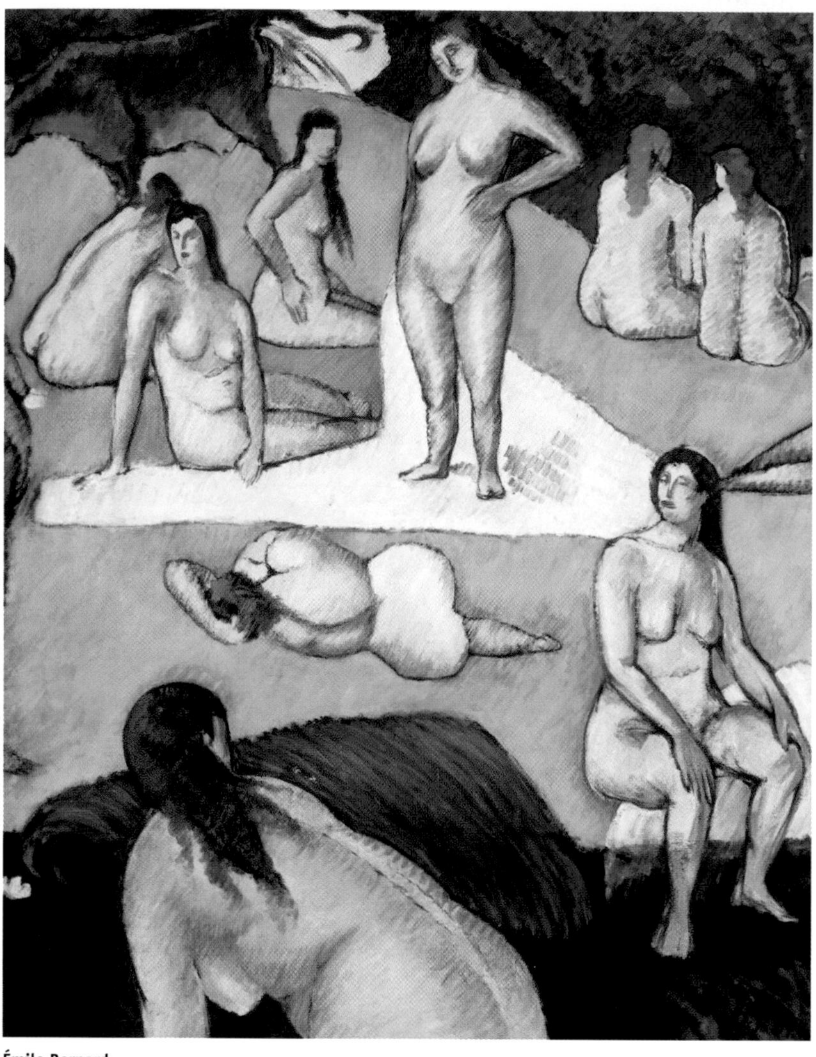

Émile Bernard,
Bathers with Red Cow,
1887, oil on canvas, 92.5 x 72.5 cm

In February 1888, having finally separated from his family a few months earlier, Gauguin decided to return to Pont-Aven. During the summer, his encounter with Émile Bernard (1868-1941), approximately twenty years his junior, would have a decisive effect on his art – he had already seen him in the same place two years previously, but had not paid him any attention. Highly influenced by Japanese prints, "petit Bernard", as he was somewhat patronisingly nicknamed by Gauguin, developed a style of painting without perspective or relief, consisting of broad, flat colours often randomly outlined with dark contours, hence the name "Cloisonnisme". In order to re-create space, he superimposed the figures which grew smaller as they moved further away. In *Bathers with Red Cow,* part of a large composition painted the year before Gauguin's arrival, Bernard once again applied all of these elements, even though the brushmarks, made up of small juxtaposed hatching, remain very reminiscent of Cézanne, whereas Cézanne's influence is much less evident in *The Harvest*, painted the following year. A few years later, Bernard wrote: "The colour... is applied pure or degraded as little as possible. Since it must determine the emotion or mental state of the painting, it is adapted to the subject; therein lies its symbolic nature. Style, distorting according to its meaning, is created by the memory left by the object which should never be copied by the artist... This is a way of painting which originates in the memory and which repeats in the mind what it has seen outside... In short, Symbolism did not paint things, but the idea of things beyond the things themselves." Émile Bernard was therefore the founder of Cloisonnisme, a title which would be usurped by Gauguin who became the leader of the school later known as "Synthetism".

Émile Bernard,
The Harvest or *Breton Landscape,*
1888, oil on canvas, 56.5 x 45 cm

Émile Bernard,
Madeleine in the Bois d'Amour,
1888, oil on canvas, 138 x 163 cm

Gauguin and Van Gogh in Arles

Vincent van Gogh,
The Dance Hall at Arles,
1888, oil on canvas, 65 x 81 cm

Gauguin complained of his lack of money in his letters to Vincent, hence Theo, a picture dealer, had the idea of bringing him to Arles, where he would support him in exchange for one painting a month. Rather reserved initially, Vincent became more and more enthusiastic: the solitude was getting him down, and he eventually dreamed of a house where several painters would work together and inspire each other. He thus decided to rent the "yellow house", which he fitted out in anticipation of Gauguin's arrival. The latter finally arrived in Arles on 23 October 1888. The two painters worked on the same subjects – Mme Ginoux (The Woman of Arles), Mme Roulin, the Sunflowers, the Washerwomen, the Alyscamps, their portraits –, usually with Gauguin taking up a subject that had already been painted by Van Gogh. Although Gaugin would have preferred a more one-sided influence, both men learned from each other, no matter what he said. In *The Dance Hall at Arles*, the flat colours, simplified forms and black outlines around the contours were inspired by Gauguin who persuaded him to paint "from memory" based on the emotions kindled by the things and the people. As for Gauguin, his vivid and occasionally random colours – the blue trunk and red spot of the bush in *The Alyscamps* – reveal Van Gogh's influence. However, the two artists, who seemed so close in their letters, were of very different dispositions, and tension began to mount. On 23 December, in a rage, Van Gogh threatened Gauguin with an open razor and then cut off his own ear. He was admitted to the general hospital the following day: during the day, he would paint outside and in the yellow house, and in the evening he would return. The neighbours became worried and soon the painter no longer left the hospital. At the beginning of May, he asked to be admitted to an asylum near Saint-Rémy-de-Provence as an "inmate". He wrote to his brother, to whom he sent his canvases: "There are a whole load of daubs inside... Now, as for me, I will never mean anything as a painter, of that I am certain."

Paul Gauguin, *The Alyscamps*, 1888,
oil on canvas, 91.5 x 72.5 cm

Paul Sérusier

End of the summer of 1888, another of Gauguin's encounters

Paul Sérusier,
Breton Eve or *Melancholy,*
circa 1890, oil on canvas, 73 x 60 cm

Paul Sérusier,
Breton Fight,
circa 1890-1891, oil on canvas, 92 x 73 cm

Born into a well-to-do Parisian family, Sérusier (1864-1927) attended the Lycée Condorcet, like Denis, Vuillard, Roussel and Lugné-Poe. In 1883, having passed his baccalauréat, he received permission from his father to enrol at the Académie Julian. Unsure of the value of his work, he made his way alone to Pont-Aven in October 1888, probably drawn by some of his friends from the Académie Julian, who had gone down to the Gloanec boarding house, where Gauguin had been staying since the winter. He spoke to Bernard first, who pointed him in the direction of Gauguin. Suffering from poor health, the latter promised to give him a painting lesson the following day. They left together for the Bois d'Amour, on the bank of the Aven, where Sérusier, practically following Gauguin's "dictation", painted a landscape on a small wooden panel – and not on the cover of a cigar case as is often believed. Maurice Denis described this event a few years later: "How do you see that tree?" asked Gaugin at a corner of the Bois d'Amour. «Green? Then paint it green, the most beautiful green on your palette. And that shadow? I would say blue. Don't be afraid of painting it as blue as possible." In comparison with classical training, this approach must have seemed revolutionary to the young art student. Without relief or shading, the landscape becomes almost abstract: abolishing perspective, random flat colours and the contours have the effect of removing all naturalistic characteristics. Without a few tree trunks and the house with its roof and gable, a landscape might not be recognisable. When he returned to Paris, Sérusier showed the painting to several of his artist friends, who soon gave the painting its title, *The Talisman*: for them, it contained the secret of a new way of painting their visual sensations. These artists would soon form a new group: the Nabis.

Paul Sérusier,
The Talisman,
1888, oil on canvas, 27 x 21.5 cm

Periods in Paris and Brittany, circa 1890

Paul Gauguin,
The Beautiful Angèle (Mme Satre),
summer 1889, oil on canvas, 92 x 73 cm

On returning from Arles, Gauguin, in Paris, started on the terrible family portrait of the "bon Schuffenecker": although the two children are lovingly handled, he spared neither of the parents. The husband, a faithful friend who would forever support Gauguin, is depicted as a small, humble creature, his hands clasped, with neither brush nor palette, standing in front of an invisible canvas, as though Gauguin wanted to deny his talent as a painter – "born to be a simple worker or concierge, or a little shopkeeper", he later declared. The wife, who is said to have rejected Gauguin and was tired of him imposing himself constantly on them in their home, was rewarded with a bitter, surly expression. Gauguin was facing hard times: the exhibition that he had arranged with friends at the Café Volpini within the precincts of the World Fair – the one with the Eiffel Tower – though not part of the event itself, was a failure. Leaving Paris again for Brittany, he settled in Pouldu, at the guesthouse run by the parents of Angèle Satre, where he met Sérusier. He decided to paint the portrait of Angèle, who was apparently regarded as the most beautiful girl in the area: "While he was working," she explained, "he would never allow me to see the canvas, because he said it was impossible to understand anything while the painting was still in progress... When he had finished, he showed it first of all to other painters who really ridiculed it, and then I knew... But when he showed it to me, I said: "How awful!" and that he could just take it away with him because I would never have that in my house... Gauguin was upset and he said, really disappointed, that he had never painted such a successful portrait before." The painter had arranged totally separate spaces next to each other, isolating the portrait in a truncated medallion outlined in ochre, a process often used in Japanese prints. The painter, who must have felt that he had expressed the essence of Breton culture, was probably disappointed by the model's reaction.

Paul Gauguin,
Still-Life with Fan,
1889, oil on canvas, 50 x 61 cm

Paul Gauguin,
Schuffenecker's Studio,
January 1889, oil on canvas, 73 x 92 cm

Vincent Van Gogh

Saint-Rémy-de-Provence, 1889

On 8 May 1889, Van Gogh was admitted to Hôpital Saint-Paul in Saint-Rémy-de-Provence of his own free will. He initially painted without leaving his room which served as his studio, and then went out into the surrounding countryside. Obsessed with his painting, he wanted to dedicate himself to it completely, but remained dissatisfied with his work. He embarked upon a new version of his *Bedroom at Arles*, destined for his mother and his sister Wil, in which elements in bright, harmonious colours are juxtaposed in a slightly smaller composition with a swinging perspective: the floor rises as if extending the wall, and the viewpoint varies according to the objects. "This time, it is simply my bedroom, only the colour should... evoke rest and sleep in general", he wrote to Theo. For him, the colours have psychological effects: they stir feelings in the onlooker. However, they also have another virtue: they enable him to define space. Since certain colours, the cold colours, like blue for example, move away from the onlooker, while the warm colours draw near to the viewer, he arranges them according to the space which he is attempting to define. "No-one yet understood that a pure tone in itself signified a certain idea of closeness or distance, wrote Francastel. A complex space may be constructed simply by juxtaposing coloured marks." At the beginning of the century, the Fauves would be able to take up the lesson once again. In his *Self-portrait*, his vivid, sinuous, tormented, spiralling brushmarks, free from the very brief influence of Gauguin and Émile Bernard, are characteristic of this period. Like his illustrious predecessor, Rembrandt, whom he infinitely admired – "Rembrandt's portraits..., they are more than nature, they are something of a revelation" –, Van Gogh painted numerous self-portraits in which he scrutinises his own face as if attempting better to know himself. "I prefer to paint human eyes rather than cathedrals", he wrote.

Vincent van Gogh,
Van Gogh's Bedroom at Arles,
1889, oil on canvas, 57.5 x 74 cm

Vincent van Gogh,
Hôpital Saint-Paul in Saint-Rémy-de-Provence,
October 1889, oil on canvas, 63 x 48 cm

Vincent van Gogh,
Meridian or *Siesta,*
after Millet,
December 1889-1890,
oil on canvas, 73 x 91 cm

Vincent van Gogh,
Portrait of the Artist,
early September 1889, oil on canvas, 65 x 54.5 cm

Haystacks as perceived by Monet and Gauguin

Claude Monet,
Haystacks, end of the summer,
1891, oil on canvas, 60.5 x 100.5 cm

Had it not been for the theme, these two paintings have nothing in common. Although he had started painting as an Impressionist, working from life using disorderly, hatched brushstrokes, Gauguin, in 1889, returning to Brittany, demonstrated a development in his work at odds with the theories of his fellow artists, as seen in *Yellow Haystacks*. In 1888, Gauguin had criticised the Impressionists for painting exclusively in the open, and with Émile Bernard he praised the virtues of working in the studio based on memory. This was the only way for the artist to gain the freedom to use whichever form or colour he chose for purely aesthetic reasons. Dating from almost the same period as Gauguin's piece, Monet's canvas is very different. During the summer of 1890, while he was living in Giverny, Monet started on a series of over twenty paintings on the theme of haystacks. His aim was clear: to re-transcribe the variable "effects" of light depending on the time the day and the season – the word "effect" moreover appears in many of the titles of the canvases in which innumerable shades of the palette aimed to convey the atmosphere and its subtle variations. Determined to set down on the canvas the most transient reality and to paint his subject as accurately as possible, Monet, paradoxically, would give a young artist an experience which would lead him to the opposite extreme of re-transcribing reality. Kandinsky told how, in 1896, upon seeing one of Monet's *haystack* paintings in Moscow for the first time, he had a real shock: he had never seen a haystack before in his life, and failed to recognise the subject. However, he was captured by the "undreamt-of power of the palette". It was partly this experience which led him towards abstract art: "I vaguely felt that the object failed the painting." Without identifying the subject, his emotion had been very strong. The greatest paradox: it was Monet who, in a way, as part of a realistic process, led Kandinsky to abstract art.

Paul Gauguin,
Yellow Haystacks or *The Golden Harvest,*
1889, oil on canvas, 73 x 92 cm

Vincent Van Gogh

A physician and a collector: Doctor Paul Gachet

Vincent van Gogh,
Mlle Gachet in the Garden,
Sunday 1 June 1890,
oil on canvas, 46 x 55.5 cm

Vincent van Gogh,
In Dr Gachet's Garden,
27 May 1890, oil on canvas, 73 x 52 cm

Paul Gachet (1828-1909) was first a doctor: he wrote his thesis on melancholy and specialised in mental illness. He was also an amateur painter and kept company with a few modest artists, whose work he collected. However, it was not until he moved to Auvers-sur-Oise, in 1872, that his collection would increase on quite a different scale. For several years, Auvers had been the home of a small artists colony and would soon, with Pissarro, become the birthplace of the new painting: Paul Cézanne and Armand Guillaumin came to stay there. Having become Pissarro's family doctor, this "indisputable leading enthusiast of new painting" became acquainted with the painters and began to collect their work. In 1889, Theo van Gogh turned to Pissarro for help in finding a place where Vincent, still in the asylum at Saint-Rémy-de-Provence, could come to live on his own. Pissarro naturally thought of Dr Gachet, who would also be able to attend to his health. On Tuesday 20 May 1890, Van Gogh moved to a café located in the square by the town hall in Auvers. "I found in Dr Gachet a friend... and something of a new brother, since we were so similar both physically and morally... He is very nervous and rather peculiar himself...", he wrote on 3 June 1890. The Gachet family was his role model: the father, of course, who was a widower, and the daughter, Marguerite. "What fascinates me most is the portrait, the modern portrait...", he wrote. "I do not attempt to paint a photographic representation, but rather our passionate expressions, using... our modern science and taste for colour. Hence, in the portrait of Dr Gachet you see a face the colour of a red-hot, sun-burnt brick, with red hair, a white hat framed by a landscape of blue hills in the background, his clothes are ultramarine blue..."

Vincent van Gogh,
Dr Paul Gachet,
beginning of June 1890, oil on canvas, 68 x 57 cm

Two churches, as perceived by Millet and Van Gogh

Jean-François Millet,
The Church at Gréville,
1871-1874, oil on canvas, 60 x 73.4 cm

When he discovered Millet's drawings and pastels, at an exhibition in Drouot in 1875, Van Gogh was deeply moved: "I felt something along the lines of "take off your shoes", for you are standing on holy ground", he wrote. He then began to collect etchings and photographs of the French painter's work, and could not rest until he started to draw. A few years later, when he read the flattering biography written by Alfred Sensier, Millet's friend and collector, Van Gogh identified with the man who was described as simple, pure and misunderstood by the rest of the world. He also saw real proof of God's existence in the scenes of peasants working in a constantly renewed nature. He produced several copies in oils of his elder's compositions, and sometimes took up the same themes: just as Millet had painted the church at Gréville in Normandy, Van Gogh painted churches on several occasions: "With that, I have a larger painting of the village church – an effect causing the building to appear purple against a simple, deep blue sky, of pure cobalt, the stained glass windows like ultramarine blue marks, the roof purple and partly orange. In the foreground, a little floral greenery and pink sun-kissed sand. It is again almost the same as the studies that I did in Nuenen [his childhood village] of the old tower and cemetery, only this time the colour is probably more expressive, more magnificent", he wrote to his sister Wilhelmine, on 5 June 1890. Although Van Gogh's brushmark and palette would no longer have anything in common with those of the French painter, Van Gogh still continued to meditate upon his work and to see in it so much evidence of "something up above".

Vincent van Gogh,
The Church at Auvers-sur-Oise, view of the chevet,
beginning of June 1890, oil on canvas, 94 x 74.5 cm

Paul Cézanne

"Imagine Poussin entirely reworked from nature"

Paul Cézanne, *Bathers,*
circa 1890-1892, oil on canvas,
60 x 82 cm

During the last fifteen years of his life, Cézanne produced views of Sainte-Victoire together with men and women bathing, the compositions of which are extremely similar. However, although he painted "series", his intention was not to study the changing light, as was the case for Monet. In his compositions on *Sainte-Victoire*, which he described as a "stunning subject", he attempted rather to express synthetically the stability of this rocky mass: the image of an unchanging massif towering towards the sky thus appears in his paintings, through coloured planes often without contours or vanishing lines, reconstructed by the onlooker, a vision devoid of all descriptive attempts. In his scenes of men and women bathing, although he admittedly revives his childhood memories of when he used to bathe and laze around on the banks of the Arc, near Aix-en-Provence with his school friends, including Zola, he above all returns to the great masters whom he had so admired and copied at the Louvre. His ambition was also to paint nudes in the middle of nature following the tradition of the figurative painters of the past: "Imagine Poussin entirely reworked from nature", he said. He defined the body with multiple facets, eventually tending towards the simplification of forms and masses, whether tree trunks or bodies. His compositions are usually very balanced: sometimes in a pyramid, sometimes in a frieze. By reducing forms to geometrical terms, by handling the space, Cézanne thus heralded the major pictorial movements of the beginning of the 20th century. His paintings no longer followed the laws of the visible, but those of aesthetic creation which reinvents space and things. "He aims to represent neither man, apple nor tree; but Cézanne uses this to create a painted thing which resonates deep within and is called the image", Kandinsky wrote in *The Art of Spiritual Harmony*.

Paul Cézanne,
La Montagne Sainte-Victoire,
circa 1890, oil on canvas, 62 x 92 cm

Paul Cézanne,
Bathers,
circa 1890-1900, oil on canvas,
22 x 33.5 cm

Vincent Van Gogh

A tragic end in Auvers-sur-Oise, 1890

Vincent van Gogh, *Thatches at Cordeville,* formerly known as *Thatches of Montcel,* end of May or beginning of June 1890, oil on canvas, 72 x 91 cm

While in Auvers, Van Gogh did not only paint the Gachet family; he also produced landscapes. On 21 May 1890, the day after his arrival, he told Theo that the place "is truly beautiful, many old thatched roofs among others, which is rare", and he described "a study of old thatched roofs, with a field of flowering peas and wheat in the foreground, and a hill in the background", perhaps referring to *Thatches at Cordeville*. Like in his canvases at Saint-Rémy, Van Gogh painted this turbulent nature which almost threatened to fall to pieces. "He had absorbed nature within himself; he had forced it to become pliable and bend to the shape of his thoughts, to follow him in his flights, even to endure his characteristic distortion... Everything, under the brush of this strange and powerful creator, is marked by a strange new life, separate from that of the things he paints, which is in him, and which is him. He puts all his energy into the trees, the sky, the flowers, the fields, which he fills with the surprising sap from his very being. These forms multiply, become dishevelled and twisted...", wrote Octave Mirbeau on 31 March 1891. The same sinuous, contorted lines create the dresses and clasped hands of the terrible portraits, *Two Little Girls*. Having fallen into a great frenzy of working, Van Gogh nevertheless continued to be racked by despondency and sadness. "Since returning to this place, I have also felt greatly saddened. My life also has been attacked at the very root, my footsteps are also faltering." On 29 July, he shot himself in the chest and died two days later: there was nothing Dr Gachet could do. A letter addressed to Theo was found in his bedroom: "... Well! I am risking my life for my work, and I seem to have half lost my reason..."

Vincent van Gogh,
Two Little Girls,
June 1890, oil on canvas, 51.2 x 51 cm

Vincent van Gogh,
Still-Life, known as
Roses and Anemones,
June 1890, oil on canvas,
51.7 x 52 cm

Paul Gauguin

Early days in Tahiti, 1891

Paul Gauguin,
Tahitian Women or *On the Beach,*
1891, oil on canvas, 69 x 91.5 cm

Brittany had not provided Gauguin with the return to primitive civilisation that he had hoped for: he continued to dream of lands far from corrupt society. "May the day come (and perhaps soon) when I will run away to an island in Oceania, to live on ecstasy, peace and art," he wrote to his wife in February 1890. "Surrounded by a new family, far from the European fight for money, there, in Tahiti, in the still of the beautiful tropical nights, I will be able to listen to the soft murmuring music of my heart in loving harmony with the mysterious beings around me." However, it took an age before he finally left: he studied the different destinations and procrastinated. In his *Journal*, the sardonic Jules Renard wrote: "Daudet, in brilliant form, told us of Gauguin's departures, that he wants to live in Tahiti to get away from people, but never leaves. It has got the point that his best friends are telling him: 'you must go, dear friend, you must go.'" Finally, in May 1891, he sailed for Tahiti from Marseille, dreaming, like Van Gogh, of establishing a brotherhood of artists. From his arrival, he found the inhabitants fascinating. While he painted one of his first Tahitian women, he wrote: "I was aware that in my study as a painter, there was a penetrating search for what lay within, like a tacit need to give oneself up, to give oneself up forever without being able to take oneself in hand again… I worked quickly, passionately." His paintings express silence, slowness, inertia, torpor, and occasionally sadness. At the same time, the large flat bright colours, which would lead the way for the riotous colours of Fauvism, evoke "the young firmness and supple heaviness of bodies ripening and stretching like plants in the sun", in the words of Charles Sterling.

Paul Gauguin, *The Meal* or *The Bananas,*
1891, oil on paper re-mounted on canvas, 73 x 92 cm

Paul Gauguin,
Arearea. Pleasantries,
1892, oil on canvas, 75 x 94 cm

Women brushing their hair under the eye of Degas and Toulouse-Lautrec

Painters were not the only ones to have been fascinated by women's hair at the end of the 19th century. Pierre Louÿs wrote *La Chevelure*, which Debussy would set to music, and certain romantic heroines would have entrancing, almost disturbing hair. Hence, in *Pelléas et Mélisande*, Maurice Maeterlinck wrote: "I have never before seen hair like yours, Mélisande! See, it is so long it flows over my heart... It even flows down to my knees... And it is so soft, as soft as if it fell from heaven!" In their scenes of women at their toilet, Degas and Toulouse-Lautrec – who greatly admired Degas – painted women brushing their hair on several occasions. In Degas' work, this naturalness and truthfulness are only outwardly observed since they result from numerous studies and sketches. His centring closes on the secret women locked away in their reverie. Toulouse-Lautrec also painted numerous anonymous women brushing their hair: he sets down a simple, graceful gesture, causing the model to be forgotten. A few years later, in 1896, in a series of lithographs entitled *Elles*, he sketched women with averted, lowered faces viewed from an overhanging perspective, captured during private moments – a woman lying down, a woman in the bathtub, a woman with a tray, a woman combing her hair, a woman in a corset... Even when the actual act of brushing their hair was not, strictly speaking, the subject of his paintings, he often emphasised his models' hair: La Goulue's chignons, Jane Avril's hats, and Cha-U-Kao's fantastic hairstyles...

Henri de Toulouse-Lautrec,
Woman Doing Her Hair, The One Who Uses a Comb,
1891, oil on cardboard, 44 x 30 cm

Edgar Degas,
Woman Combing Her Hair,
circa 1890-1892, pastel, 82 x 52 cm

Comparison of works

The "Modern Painters" and women at their toilet

Edgar Degas,
The Bathtub, 1886, pastel on cardboard, 60 x 83 cm, 8th Impressionist Exhibition, 1886

Edgar Degas,
Woman Getting out of the Bath, 1877, pastel on monotype, 16 x 21.5 cm, 3rd Impressionist Exhibition, 1877

Edgar Degas,
Cup of Chocolate After the Bath, circa 1905-1908, pastel and charcoal, 113 x 111 cm

At the final Impressionist Exhibition in 1886, Edgar Degas showed a series of ten pastels entitled "Series of female nudes bathing, washing, drying themselves, combing their hair or having it combed for them", which included *The Bathtub*, one of Degas' most famous pastels of a woman at her toilet; from this time on, the artist would repeatedly return to this theme, capturing his model from every angle and reconstructing, pastel by pastel, the sequence of movements, like a film, often viewed from above, in the style of Cézanne's last still-lives. In Degas' work, the figures of ordinary, anonymous women absorbed in their task, are mostly seen from the back, the face either hidden or indistinct. They are naked, but not provocatively so, as though they are unaware that they are being watched. Their poses make them vulnerable rather than sensual. Degas explained to the Irish writer George Moore: "Until now, the nude has always been depicted in poses suggesting an audience, but my women are simple, honest people attending to nothing more than their physical existence. This is one of them: she is washing her feet. It is as if you were looking through the keyhole." Degas increasingly used pastels over time, a rapid technique which helped him to avoid straining his eyes – during the 18th century, Chardin also used this technique towards the end of his life. Toulouse-Lautrec, who greatly admired Degas, took up the theme of women at their toilet, also adopting an overhang-ing perspective, centring which intersects the composition and gives the glimpsed scenes their immediacy. Seen from behind with infinite respect and modesty, *the Redhead*, in the privacy of her décor, seems to be unaware that she is being observed: he succeeds in making one forget that a model had nonetheless posed for him in order to reconstruct life.

Berthe Morisot, *Young Woman Powdering Her Face*, 1877, oil on canvas, 46 x 39 cm

Edgar Degas,
After the Bath, Woman Rubbing Her Neck,
circa 1895, pastel,
62.2 x 65 cm

Edgar Degas,
Naked Woman Crouching, From the Back,
circa 1876-1877,
pastel, 18 x 14 cm

Edgar Degas,
After the Bath or *Naked Woman Lying Down* or Nude Lying Down, circa 1885,
pastel, 48 x 87 cm

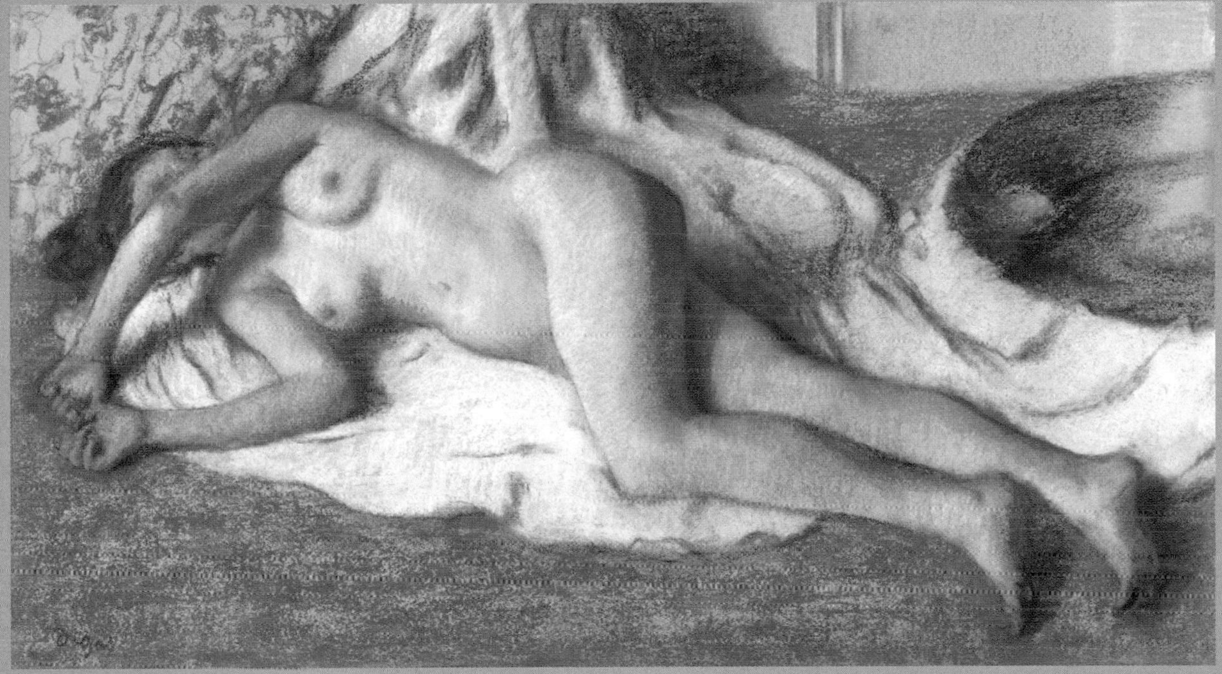

Edgar Degas,
Woman at her Toilet, Wiping her Left Foot, circa 1885-1886,
pastel on cardboard, 54.3 x 52.4 cm

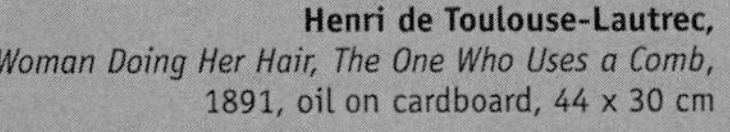

Henri de Toulouse-Lautrec,
Woman Doing Her Hair, The One Who Uses a Comb,
1891, oil on cardboard, 44 x 30 cm

Henri de Toulouse-Lautrec,
Woman at Her Toilet or *Redhead,*
1896, oil on cardboard, 67 x 54 cm

Paul Signac

A new leader

Paul Signac,
Woman in Lamplight,
1890, oil on wood,
24 x 15 cm

Paul Signac,
Green Sail, Venice,
1904, oil on canvas,
65 x 81 cm

Paul Signac,
Woman at the Well. Opus 238,
1892, oil on canvas,
194.8 x 130.7 cm

When Seurat died in 1891, his friend Signac was altogether suited to taking up the torch: the latter then used brushmarks divided into small juxtaposed dots of pure colour and thus finally moved away from the "romantic impressionism" of a Monet or Sisley, in order to embark upon "scientific impressionism". A few years later, he undertook to draw up a posteriori a treatise on Neo-Impressionism, entitled *D'Eugène Delacroix au néo-impressionnisme* published in 1899. Like many other artists, Signac was drawn by the light of the South, and moved to Saint-Tropez, then an unknown small village, to a house called La Hune. He often invited his artist friends there, such as Cross, who lived nearby in Cabasson, Maximilien Luce, Theo van Rysselberghe and, later, Henri Matisse, together with the critic Fénéon, an early, ardent defender of the Neo-Impressionist movement – he was also responsible for giving the movement its name. The sheltered bay of Saint-Tropez was also for Signac, who was an excellent sailor, an ideal place to moor his boat, which took him on numerous cruises in the Mediterranean. As time went by, Signac moved away from the rigorous principles of Neo-Impressionism: in his landscapes, which became his single subject, he broke away from small dots adopting a larger, freer brushmark, which brought him back to his original master, Monet. In *Red Buoy*, his brushmarks, which had become more square in shape and were arranged less tightly, made his canvas more spontaneous, expressive and lyrical. It is a remarkable fact that many young artists, who would bring fame to the more innovative movements at the beginning of the 20th century, would go through a brief Neo-Impressionist period, from the Italian Futurists to Henri Matisse and Robert Delaunay.

Paul Signac,
Red Buoy,
1895, oil on canvas, 81 x 65 cm

Claude Monet

Hour by hour, season by season: the Rouen Cathedral series

Claude Monet,
Rouen Cathedral, Main Door, Front View, Harmony of Browns,
1892, oil on canvas, 107 x 73 cm

Claude Monet,
Rouen Cathedral, Main Door and Saint-Romain Tower, Morning Effect, Harmony of Whites,
1893, oil on canvas, 106 x 73 cm

Claude Monet,
Rouen Cathedral, Main Door and Saint-Romain Tower, Full Sun, Harmony of Blue and Gold,
1893, oil on canvas, 107 x 73 cm

Monet's vast correspondence makes it possible to understand how he approached this cathedral series during two visits to Rouen, one in 1892, and the other in 1893. "... I have been able to set up in an empty apartment opposite the cathedral, but it is going to be a tough job", he wrote to his wife in February 1892. On 3 April 1892: "... Every day I add and detect something that I had not yet been able to see... It is very difficult, but it is working, and a few more days of this beautiful sun, and a good number of my canvases will be saved. I am exhausted, I can't stand it any longer, and... I had nightmares all night long: the cathedral was falling on me, it appeared blue or pink or yellow." He finished the thirty or so cathedrals in the studio; the subject is identical – the western façade of the monument –, whereas in the *Haystacks* series it varied from one painting to another. Only the viewpoint changes. However, his attention is drawn to the infinite variations in the atmosphere and light on the stone façade with the passing hours and days. "With twenty canvases, with various precisely chosen effects, the painter gives the impression that he could have or should have painted fifty, one hundred, one thousand of them, as many as the number of seconds in his life, if he lived as long as the stone monument", Clemenceau wrote in the long article dedicated to the artist in *La Justice* on 20 May 1895..." The wonder of Monet's sensation lies in watching the stone vibrating and in conveying it to us with all its resonance... That is without mentioning the technical nature of the colours. Looking at Monet's cathedrals close up, it seems as though they were made of some kind of versicolour mortar ground onto the canvas in a fit of rage. This wild behaviour stems from passion, without a doubt, but also from science. How can the artist just a few centimetres from his canvas be aware of both a precise and subtle effect that can only be appreciated from a distance? This is the disconcerting mystery of his retinal screen."

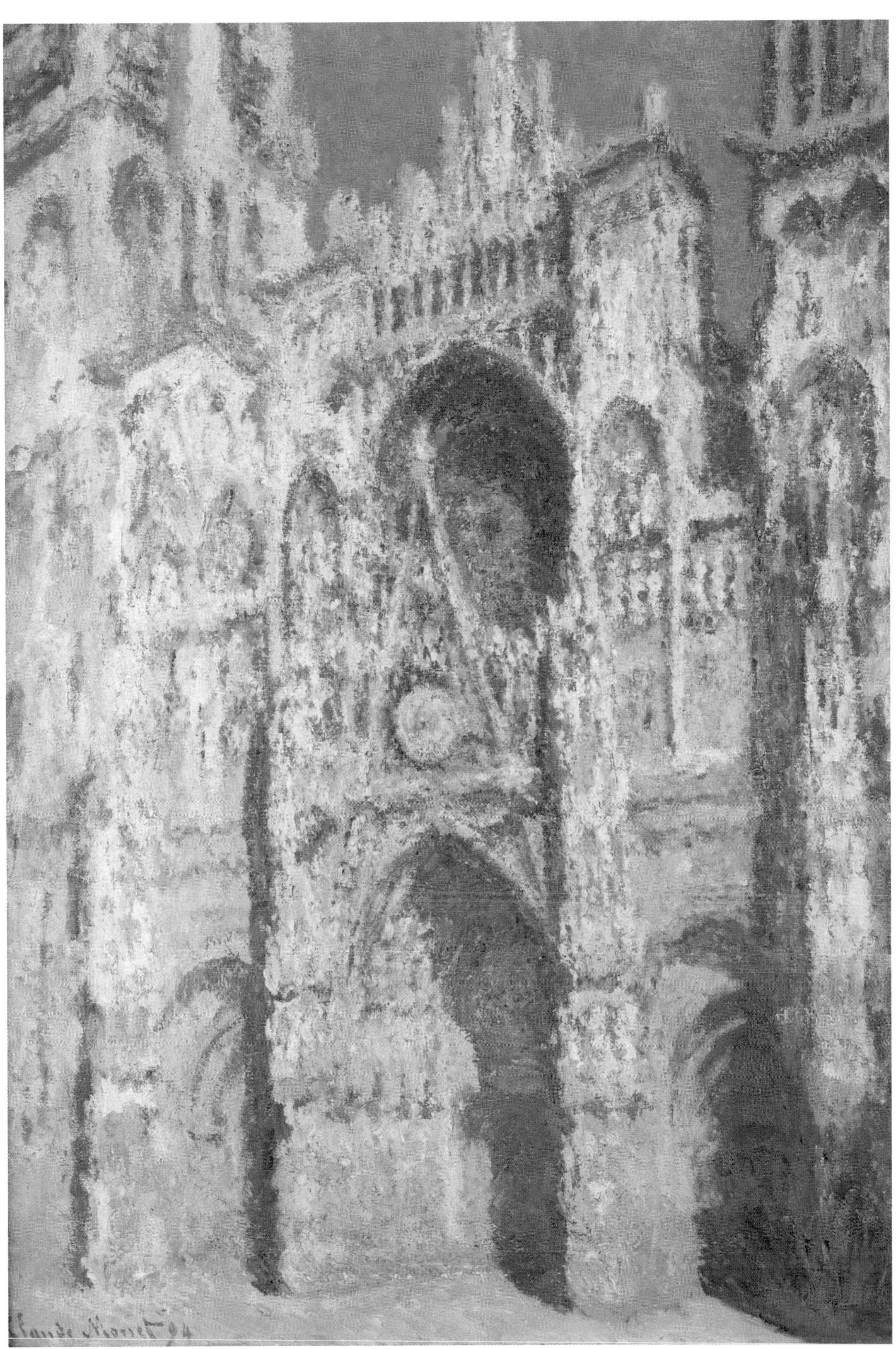

In his own eyes, Gauguin was first a painter

Paul Gauguin, *Self-Portrait with Yellow Christ*, 1890-1891, oil on canvas, 38 x 46 cm

With an identical, small format, these two self-portraits painted before and after Gauguin's visit to Tahiti are unbiased, when compared with photographs from the period. The three-quarter length pose, similar, even though the centring is not as tight as the second, emphasises the painter's features: narrow forehead, bent nose, thin lips, slightly drooping eyelids, gaze fixed on the onlooker, a heavy, bony, tense, almost impenetrable face. In both cases, the background is filled with Gauguin's work: he portrays himself as a painter and sculptor, like other great painters before him. In the first, the artist's head is outlined on two of his recent works. On the left is part of the *Yellow Christ*, which he had painted in the autumn of 1889, near to Pont-Aven, though the wrong way round – Gauguin used a mirror in order to paint the canvas. The figure of Christ associated with that of the painter is a recurring theme in his work, as though he identified with Christ – Gauguin the martyr, sacrificing himself to painting –, while placing himself under the protection of his open arms. On the right, *The Tobacco Jar made of enamelled stoneware,* the right way round this time since it was painted from a photograph, which he himself described as "vaguely representing a head of the wild Gauguin", and which symbolises his primitive, solitary being. The second self-portrait shows, on the right, a painting produced in Tahiti, *Manao Tupapau*, again the wrong way round, which Gauguin considered one of his better pieces. The two portraits are also similar in their palette, with yellow, Gauguin's mascot colour, and blue, even though the presence of the two colours is more assertive in the first portrait. However, the brushstrokes distinguish the two pieces the most: Cézanne's influence is still very marked in the first canvas, with the parallel coloured hatching.

Paul Gauguin,
Self-portrait with Hat,
winter 1893-1894, oil on canvas,
46 x 38 cm

Paul Cézanne

"The culmination of art is the figure"

Paul Cézanne,
Portrait of Mme Cézanne,
1888-1890, oil on canvas, 47 x 39 cm

Paul Cézanne,
Gustave Geffroy,
1895-1896, oil on canvas, 110 x 89 cm,
Salon d'Automne, 1907

"The culmination of art is the figure", Cézanne apparently said to the picture dealer Vollard. When Mme Cézanne, who was easily her husband's main female model, grew impatient with the never-ending sitting sessions, the painter would reply: "Do the apples move?" This was because Cézanne above all feared losing, due to his model's movement, what he referred to as his "minute sensation", which he obtained after hours and hours of observation. Many of his subjects – some famous but also anonymous ordinary people – told of his incredible concentration, and his disappointment or near despair of not finding the exact brushmark. Ambroise Vollard, who endured approximately one hundred and fifteen sitting sessions, each lasting two or three hours, recounted: "It is difficult to imagine the extent to which, on certain days, his work was slow and tiresome. In my portrait, there are two small dots on the hand where the canvas was not covered. I pointed this out to Cézanne: 'Try to understand, Monsieur Vollard, if I put something there haphazardly, I would be obliged to work on the whole painting again starting from that particular point.'" Gustave Geffroy, art critic and writer, would tolerate eighty sitting sessions... all for an unfinished painting. In *Woman with Coffee-Pot*, Cézanne brilliantly illustrates his famous precept, "handle nature using the cylinder, the sphere and the cone": a cylinder for the coffee-pot and the cup, a pyramid for the seated figure, and a square pattern for the double doors. Despite the reduction of forms to geometrical terms, the final impression fluctuates between balance and instability. Although a few details convey some of the model's psychological characteristics – for example, the knot in the sash evokes meticulousness –, for Cézanne, a portrait is also a set of coloured areas which must be arranged both justifiably and in accordance with nature. Painting is "harmony in parallel with nature": it does not attempt to convey reality, but creates a new reality.

Paul Cézanne,
Woman with Coffee-Pot,
circa 1890-1895, oil on canvas, 130.5 x 96.5 cm

Paul Sérusier, Maurice Denis and Ker-Xavier Roussel

From the Pont-Aven School to the Nabis

Paul Sérusier,
The Shower,
1893, oil on canvas,
73.5 x 60 cm

On returning to Paris from Brittany, Paul Sérusier showed his friends at the Académie Julian *The Talisman*, "this landscape, shapeless through being synthetically formulated", as described by Maurice Denis. Some of them were fascinated by this new way of painting and they soon formed a kind of brotherhood which challenged the lessons given by their professors. The following artists thus united around Sérusier: Maurice Denis, Ker-Xavier Roussel, Paul Ranson, Henri-Gabriel Ibels, Georges Lacombe, Jan Verkade, Édouard Vuillard and Pierre Bonnard: these were the Nabis – *nabi*, which, in Hebrew, means "prophet". Mostly aged in their twenties, they were fascinated by religious and philosophical issues, together with theatre and music, and dreamed of reforming art. In the summer of 1890, one of them, Maurice Denis (1870-1943), defined the principles of the Nabi style in an article-cum-manifesto in which he wrote a phrase which would become famous in the history of modern painting: "It must be remembered that a painting – before becoming a battle horse, a naked woman, or any other anecdote – is essentially a flat surface covered with colours assembled in a certain order." Denis no longer therefore questioned the means of painting, but gave a new definition of a picture and indicated a new way of approaching painting: if nature always serves as a subject of inspiration, the painter will convey his impressions through formal, colour equivalents. The paint-ing will therefore primarily stand out because of its pictorial qualities. "Expressive synthesis, the symbol of a sensation must be an eloquent transcription of this, and at the same time an object created to be pleasing to the eye." This aesthetic approach, which perceives the painting as an object in itself, foreshadowed the major pictorial movements of the beginning of the 20th century: Cubism and abstract art.

Ker-Xavier Roussel,
The Terrace,
circa 1892-1893, oil on canvas,
36 x 75 cm

Maurice Denis,
The Muses,
1893, oil on canvas,
171.5 x 137.5 cm

Maurice Denis,
Homage to Cézanne,
1900, oil on canvas, 180 x 240 cm.
Left to right: Redon, Vuillard, Mellerio, Vollard, Denis, Sérusier, Ranson, Roussel, Bonnard and Mme Denis, around a still-life by Cézanne, *Fruit Bowl, Glass and Apples* which belonged to Gauguin

Pierre Bonnard and Édouard Vuillard

The Nabis, a group of friends

Pierre Bonnard,
Portrait of Vuillard,
1892, oil on wood,
14.5 x 21.8 cm

Édouard Vuillard met Ker-Xavier Roussel (1867-1944) at the Lycée Condorcet in 1879. Both students attended courses by Diogène Maillart, a Prix de Rome laureate and a friend of Roussel's father. They were then reunited at the Académie Julian, and again in the Nabis group, and exhibited together. They became even closer by the marriage, in 1893, of Ker-Xavier Roussel, a great seducer, to Vuillard's sister. Bonnard and Vuillard met at the École des Beaux-Arts. In 1891, they shared with Maurice Denis the cramped studio belonging to Lugné-Poe, director of the Théâtre de l'Œuvre, situated at number 28 rue Pigalle. The Swiss artist, Vallotton, became acquainted with the Nabis in around 1892. Vallotton was probably closest to Vuillard: they remained friends throughout their lives, even after Vallotton joined the ranks of the Parisian upper middle classes through his marriage in 1899, as shown in their regular correspondence. Admittedly, the Nabis would only exist as part of a group for a few years: although they exhibited together regularly during the 1890s at the Indépendants, Le Barc de Bouteville and Vollard's, and would meet in the offices of *La Revue blanche* with its writers whose names would soon become prestigious –

Édouard Vuillard,
Ker-Xavier Roussel,
known as *Man Reading,*
circa 1890-1891, oil on wood,
35 x 19 cm

Édouard Vuillard,
Portrait of Félix Vallotton,
1900, oil on cardboard embedded into wood,
63 x 49.5 cm

Jules Renard, André Gide, Verlaine, Apollinaire, Claudel, Péguy, Jarry, Proust... –, from the beginning of the 1900s, each of them followed their own path and developed their own personality, while the major innovative movements in the early 20th century followed one after the other: "... the march of progress increased its pace," declared Bonnard. "Society was ready to accept Cubism and Surrealism before we had achieved our aims. We found ourselves in some way suspended in mid air." The bonds of friendship uniting the painters would nevertheless stand the test of time.

Pierre Bonnard

A "Japanese Nabi"

Pierre Bonnard,
Child Playing in the Sand, also known as *Child with Bucket,* circa 1894, tempera mixed with glue on canvas, 167 x 50 cm, panel of a folding screen

Within the Nabi group, all of the artists retained their own personality, which is strongly suggested by their nicknames. While Maurice Denis, a convinced catholic, was described as the "Nabi of the beautiful icons" and Sérusier as the "Nabi with the glowing red beard", Pierre Bonnard (1867-1947) was the "Japanese Nabi": the exhibition of Japanese etchings organised at the École des Beaux-Arts in Paris in the spring of 1890 had a lasting effect on the pictorial research of this lawyer who attended the Académie Julian. This was where he met Sérusier, Ranson and Denis; the latter introduced him to Vuillard in 1890, with whom he remained very close throughout his life. Bonnard then took part in developing the Nabi aesthetic, visited the "Temple", Ranson's studio, where all the painters would regularly meet, and exhibited with them. The Japanese influence took on several forms: subjects taken from everyday life, off-centre compositions, overhanging perspective, and the taste for decorative detail taken so far as to distort the subjects as a means of expression. In *The White Cat,* inspired by Japanese feline images, the disproportionate paws of the cat arching its back, its tail drawing a large S, its eyes reduced to two lines and its drawn-back head characterise the sensuality and feline essence of the animal. In *The Checked Blouse*, which is indeed the portrait of the painter's sister, the title of which evokes the subject that he wanted to illustrate, the importance of the check pattern of the blouse, the long narrow format and the absence of relief are taken straight from Japanese prints. "M. Bonnard paints in a very personal Japanese style", Maurice Denis wrote in *La Revue blanche* on the subject of *Twilight*, exhibited at the 8th Salon des Artistes indépendants in 1892.

Pierre Bonnard,
The Checked Blouse,
1892, oil on canvas, 61 x 33 cm

Pierre Bonnard,
The White Cat,
1894, oil on cardboard,
51 x 33 cm

Pierre Bonnard,
Twilight or *The Game of Croquet,*
1892, oil on canvas, 130 x 162.5 cm,
8th Salon des Artistes indépendants, 1892

Édouard Vuillard

Another Nabi, known as the "Zouave"

Édouard Vuillard,
Profile of Woman with Green Hat,
circa 1891, oil on cardboard, 21 x 16 cm

Édouard Vuillard,
Self-Portrait,
circa 1889, oil on canvas,
24.5 x 19 cm

Although he did not yet know it, Édouard Vuillard (1868-1940) would soon be reunited with his young friends from the Lycée Condorcet, Maurice Denis and Ker-Xavier Roussel at the Académie Julian. It was, moreover, the latter who convinced him to abandon his military career – hence his nickname "Zouave". In 1890, thanks to Denis, he met Bonnard and Sérusier, and thus became part of the Nabi group, even though, at the start, he felt rather distant from his companions' "anti-naturalistic" stance. He was finally won over in 1891. He rented a studio which he shared with Bonnard at 28 rue Pigalle. Within the Nabi group, he formed a circle with Bonnard and Roussel, which moved slightly away from the others, less fascinated than Sérusier, Ranson, Verkade and Denis by religious issues. Like Bonnard, this rather unassuming man took his subjects from everyday life: he portrayed those closest to him, the women in his family and the seamstresses in the dressmaking workroom which took up part of their apartment – Vuillard's mother lived with her son her whole life. In his work dating from the 1890s, in which he explored numerous techniques, Vuillard, also influenced by Japanese prints, created canvases without depth or relief, in which the flat colours outlined with undulating contours represented so many plastic equivalents expressing emotions. In his preface to the 9th Nabi Exhibition in 1895, Maurice Denis wrote: "In their work, they favoured expression through décor, through the harmony of forms and colours, through the material used, rather than expression through the subject. They believed that for every emotion, for every human thought, a decorative, plastic equivalent exists, with matching beauty."

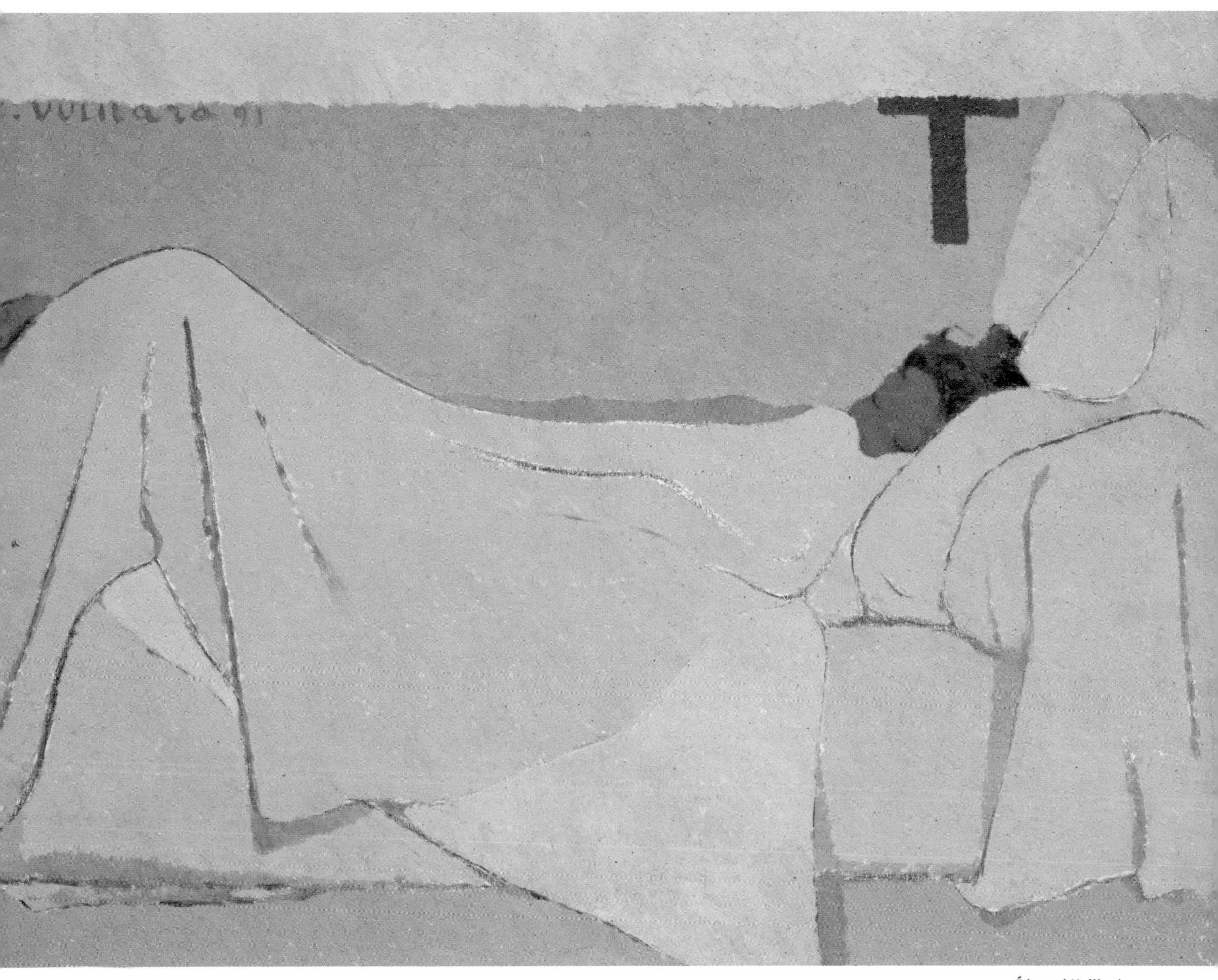

Édouard Vuillard,
In Bed, 1891, oil on canvas,
74 x 92.5 cm

Decorative panels painted by Bonnard and Vuillard

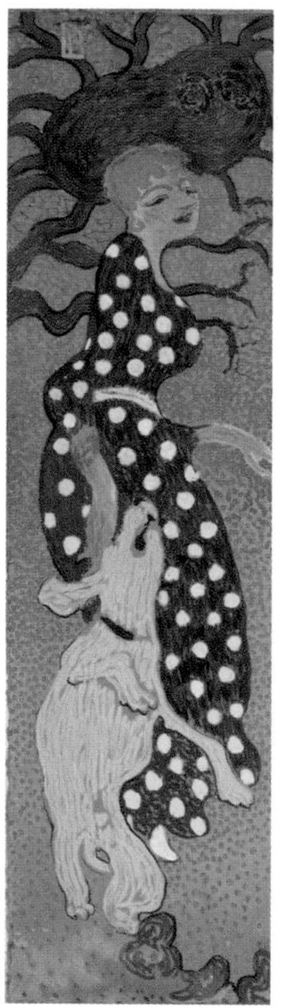

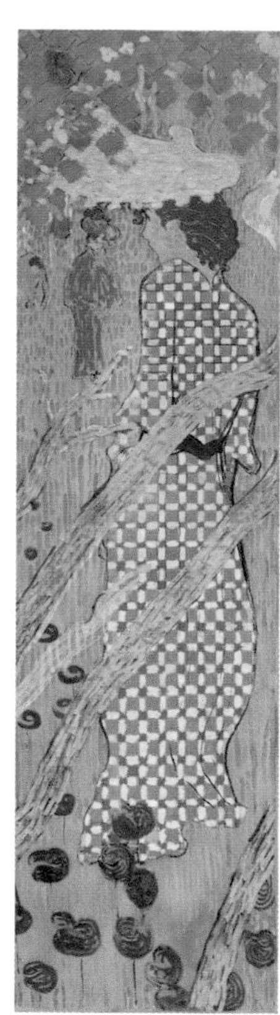

Pierre Bonnard,
Women in the Garden,
1891, tempera on paper re-mounted on canvas, 160 x 48 cm:
Woman in a White Polka Dot Dress,
Seated Woman with Cat,
Woman with Checked Dress,
Woman with Cape

"Towards the beginning of 1890, a battle cry was raised, going from one studio to another: no more easel paintings!... The work of a painter starts where that of an architect seemingly ends. Walls should remain surfaces, they should not be broken by images of endless horizons. There are no paintings, only decorations", wrote Jan Verkade, one of the first Nabis who then joined the Benedictines. Though perhaps a little extreme, these words adequately describe the attraction of the Nabis for the decorative arts and their desire to abolish all hierarchy between the arts. These painters went on to illustrate literary works and magazines, and to design posters – Bonnard's *France-Champagne* poster, which covered the walls of the capital in 1891, won him instant fame – together with theatre sets and programmes, particularly for their friend Lugné-Poe, director of the Théâtre de l'Œuvre. Close friends of numerous writers – Maurice Maeterlinck, Alfred Jarry, Oscar Wilde –, they dreamed of an art incorporated into architecture and, like Wagner, desired to create "total works of art" which made use of all the different arts. "I personally had the idea of popular goods with ordinary uses: engravings, furniture, fans, folding screens, etc.", Bonnard maintained. Bonnard and Vuillard were pioneers in the field of decorative arts among the Nabis. In March 1891, Bonnard presented the first decorative Nabi collection, *Women in the Garden*, with the vague title "Decorative panels 1-2-3-4". These were originally designed as the panels of a folding screen, in which the silhouettes without shading or relief, defined by arabesques, were tacked on to a random, flat space. In 1894, Alexandre Natanson commissioned nine panels on the theme of *Public Gardens* from Vuillard, to decorate his dining-room. Vuillard thus used paint mixed with glue for aesthetic reasons: being more matt, it avoided the illusions of oil paints.

Édouard Vuillard,
Public Gardens, 1894:
decorative panels commissioned by Alexandre Natanson
for the dining-room of his hotel situated at 60 avenue du Bois,
now avenue Foch, in Paris, paint mixed with glue on canvas:
Little Girls Playing, 214.5 x 88 cm,
Questions, 214.5 x 92 cm,
The Nannies, 213.5 x 73 cm,
The Conversation, 213 x 154 cm,
Red Umbrella, 214 x 81 cm

Comparison of works

The Nabis and feminine intimacy

Félix Vallotton,
Interior Scene, Woman Taking off Her Chemise, 1900, oil on cardboard, 55.5 x 30.5 cm

Félix Vallotton,
Interior, Woman in Blue Looking in a Cupboard,
1903, oil on canvas, 81 x 46 cm

Pierre Bonnard,
Woman at Her Toilet, circa 1908, oil on canvas, 119 x 79 cm

"Nowhere else, apart from in his illustrations of Verlaine's *Parallèlement*, has Bonnard pushed his sense of voluptuous pleasure so far. In terms of sensuality, these canvases exceed Fragonard, they exceed Courbet, they exceed Manet... May this not sound false, may it ring true", John Russel wrote with regard to *Woman Asleep on a Bed*, painted by Bonnard in 1899. The same intimist atmosphere surrounds *Man and Woman*, a canvas painted a year later, in which natural, everyday life overrides eroticism: the tall vertical line of the screen irreparably separates the man and the woman, and emphasises their solitude. The centring which cuts the two figures on each side enhances the instantaneous nature of this intimate moment. In 1893, Bonnard met a woman with a slender figure, long legs, and small, pert, firm breasts: this was Maria Boussin – he preferred to call her Marthe – who often served as his model and whom he married a few years later. It was this imperfect body, both sensual and vulnerable, which he painted in his famous bathroom nudes from the 1920s, a constantly recurring theme until his death. Although nudes are present to a lesser extent in Vuillard's work, he also painted numerous serene intimate scenes, often in small formats with muted cold, in which women seen from behind or a three-quarter view are captured in insignificant activities; sometimes they are simply asleep. Also influenced by Japanese prints, Vuillard applied matt, flat colours in a space without perspective, in which the figures seem to disappear into the wall. From the outset, Vallotton also painted intimate scenes in which eroticism occasionally, coldness and Realism always, are aided by a smooth technique conveying an almost bitter vision of the world and its creatures.

Édouard Vuillard,
*Two Women Sewing,*1912, resumed in 1933,
oil on canvas, 201 x 113.5 cm

Pierre Bonnard,
Blue Nude,
circa 1899-1900,
oil on wood,
30 x 39.5 cm

Pierre Bonnard,
Woman Asleep on a Bed,
also known as *Idle Nude,*
1899, oil on canvas, 96 x 106 cm,
Munich, Sezession, 1907-1908

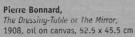

Pierre Bonnard,
Man and Woman,
1900, oil on canvas, 115 x 72.5 cm

Maurice Denis,
Nude. Woman Seated, from behind,
1891, pastel and charcoal, 73 x 57 cm

Pierre Bonnard,
Interior or *Woman with Dog,*
circa 1920, oil on canvas, 53 x 57 cm

Pierre Bonnard,
The Dressing-Table or *The Mirror,*
1908, oil on canvas, 52.5 x 45.5 cm

Édouard Vuillard,
The Linen Cupboard,
circa 1893-1895, oil on cardboard, 25 x 20 cm

Paul Cézanne

On either side of a bottle

Paul Cézanne, *The Card Players,* circa 1890-1895, oil on canvas, 47 x 57 cm

A painting from the school of the Le Nain brothers, *The Card Players*, at the Musée Granet, in Aix-en-Provence, is said to have given Cézanne the idea of illustrating the same theme. However, unlike the 17th-century painters who, in the tradition of Caravaggio, had presented an anecdotal or moralist version of the scene – as seen in *The Cheat* by Georges de La Tour, Cézanne stripped away all elements of a genre scene in order to transform it into an exercise on line and volume. He produced five paintings together with numerous preliminary drawings and watercolours. As he painted the successive versions, he gradually reduced the format of the canvas, eliminated the remaining anecdotal details and reduced the number of onlookers and players. The five figures standing or sitting in the earlier versions were reduced to four, and then finally two players sitting on either side of a table, as seen in the painting at the Musée d'Orsay. The palette was likewise reduced to monochrome ochres. On either side of a vertical bottle moved slightly over to the right, counterbalanced by the horizontal lines of the table and panelling, two men – two farm labourers from Jas de Bouffan, Cézanne's family estate – have taken their places at opposite ends of the table, solitary and silent, motionless and concentrating hard. The game has not yet begun, the players still hold all the cards. The same geometrical composition is used in *Still-Life with Onions*, in which the bottle and glass mark the vertical axis of the composition: the edge of the table traces the horizontal line, while the knife creates depth. Unlike the later still-lives, the background here is totally empty – it would become considerably more crowded as the years went by.

Paul Cézanne,
Still-Life with Onions,
circa 1895, oil on canvas, 66 x 82 cm

Paul Cézanne,
Study for one of the Card Players,
between 1870 and 1892, oil on canvas, 50.2 x 46.2 cm

Paul Gauguin

Farewell to Europe forever

Paul Gauguin,
Peasant Women,
1894, oil on canvas, 66 x 92.5 cm

In Tahiti, Gauguin felt isolated, his health deteriorated and he found himself penniless: he decided to return to France. On 30 August 1893, when he landed at Marseille, he did not realise that this would be his last visit to Europe. On 10 November 1893, an exhibition of his Tahiti canvases opened at the Galerie Durand-Ruel. Although Octave Mirbeau described the pieces as having "supreme grace, deep fear, intellectual irony and admirable colours", this was an exceptional opinion since the work mainly aroused derision: "If you would like to amuse your children, send them to Gauguin's exhibition. They will have fun in front of the colourful images, representing quadrumanous females, lying on billiard cloths, the whole thing accompanied with words in the local dialect." Even painters – with the exception of Degas – and writers showed their scepticism, and Gauguin was obliged to buy back thirty-nine of the forty-nine canvases exhibited. Hoping to be recognised at last, he felt misunderstood and excluded. In the summer of 1894, he decided to return to Brittany, a place which a few years earlier had represented a return to the simple life. However, a brawl in the port of Concarneau turned out badly: an open fracture confined him to bed for three months at the Gloanec boarding house. As a result, he painted very little. "This whole chain of misfortunes, the difficulty in earning a *regular* living despite my reputation, helped on by my love for the exotic have caused me to make an irrevocable decision", Gauguin wrote in September 1894. "This is what I have decided: in December I will return and I will work each day to sell everything I own, either in one lot or in parts. Once I have obtained the capital, I will return to Oceania... There is nothing to stop me from leaving and this time it will be for good." He again dreamed of leaving with a few other artists, but he would once again depart for the Tropics alone, in poor health and in despair, at the age of forty-seven.

Paul Gauguin,
Brittany Landscape, Le Moulin David,
1894, oil on canvas, 73 x 92 cm

Paul Gauguin,
Breton Village in the Snow,
1894, oil on canvas, 62 x 87 cm

Henri de Toulouse-Lautrec
"Official painter to La Goulue"

Henri de Toulouse-Lautrec,
Dancing at the Moulin-Rouge
or *La Goulue and Valentin le Désossé,*
1895, oil on canvas, 298 x 316 cm,
panel for La Goulue's booth,
at the Foire du Trône in Paris

Montmartre, with its dance halls, brothels and cafés was one of Toulouse-Lautrec's favourite themes. The artistes he frequented there were known as Yvette Guilbert, Loïe Fuller, Jane Avril and, of course, La Goulue – in 1893, *Le Figaro illustré* described him as "official painter to La Goulue". This little laundry woman, whose real name was Louise Weber, first made a name for herself at the Moulin de la Galette, and then at the Moulin-Rouge when it opened in 1889. In April 1895, as her success waned, she decided – then aged only twenty-nine – to set up in a booth at the Foire du Trône and asked the artist to paint two panels which would flank the entrance. "My dear friend, I will visit you on the 8th of April, at two o'clock in the afternoon, my booth will be at the Trône where I have been placed to the left of the entrance, I have been given a very good place and I would be very grateful if you had the time to paint something for me; tell me where I should go to purchase my canvases, and I will give them to you in the course of the day." The

Henri de Toulouse-Lautrec,
The Moorish Dance or *The Egyptian Dancing Girls,*
1895, oil on canvas, 285 x 307.5 cm,
panel for La Goulue's booth,
at the Foire du Trône in Paris, with (from left to right),
Paul Sescau, Maurice Guibert, Gabriel Tapié
de Ceyleran, Oscar Wilde, Jane Avril,
Toulouse-Lautrec and Félix Fénéon

first panel represents the lanky silhouette of Valentin le Désossé whose hand is too big and neck too long, playing opposite La Goulue standing firmly on her feet, from the days of the Moulin Rouge. The second panel portrays her in her act at the Foire du Trône, surrounded by Toulouse-Lautrec's friends: Gabriel Tapié de Céleyran, his cousin, Oscar Wilde, Félix Fénéon and Jane Avril. The latter, an elegant, cultured woman, described him as "the brilliant cripple" and posed for him on several occasions. "In the middle of the crowd," related Paul Leclercq, "there was a stir and a line formed: Jane Avril was dancing, turning, graceful and light, a little eccentric, pale and slender, a thoroughbred." This portrait of "the embodiment of dance" demonstrates the dazzling technique of the artist, who applied his colour directly with the brush: the face, a true portrait, and upper part of the body are painted with energetic, precise brushstrokes, while the rest of the painting is barely sketched, and the texture of the canvas remains largely visible.

Henri de Toulouse-Lautrec,
Jane Avril Dancing,
circa 1892, oil on cardboard, 85.5 x 45 cm

Paul Gauguin at the end of the 1890s

Further away, and still further: Tahiti and the Marquesas Islands

Paul Gauguin,
Vairumati,
1897, oil on canvas, 73 x 94 cm

Paul Gauguin,
Their Glowing Golden Bodies,
1901, oil on canvas, 67 x 76 cm

Embittered and already worn-out by syphilis, Gauguin landed in Tahiti in September 1895. However, he no longer experienced the wonder that he had first felt on discovering these lands a few years previously. His despair was such that he attempted, or so it seemed to him, to commit suicide: "... I am nothing, if not a failure", he wrote to Daniel de Monfreid in April 1896, and in September 1897: "My trip to Tahiti was an insane but sad and wretched adventure." It was nevertheless during this period of physical and moral despair that he painted some magnificent pieces symbolising youth and idyllic happiness. Vairumati, a legendary figure of the Maori people, is sitting on a bed, her torso emphasised by the lavishly decorated gilded frame which serves as a kind of halo. Next to her, a bird clutches a lizard in its talons, perhaps symbolising the eternal return of desire and death. They reappear in the left of the large composition that he painted the same year and which he perceived as his legacy piece, *Where Do We Come from? Who Are We? Where Are We Going?*, in Boston. In *The White Horse*, which had been rejected by its initial recipient due to the colour of the horse – "But the horse is green! There is no such thing as a green horse" –, the two riders hidden behind the branches and the drinking horse again give the image of a luxuriant, idyllic nature in which man lives in perfect harmony. However, Gauguin remained dissatisfied and dreamed of distant, even more remote lands: "I believe that in the Marquesas Islands, since models are so easy to find... and with new landscapes to discover – in brief, completely new and even wilder elements, I will be able to make some beautiful things. Here, my imagination is beginning to cool off..." It was there that he would paint some of his finest pieces with remarkable detail and energy, such as *Their Glowing Golden Bodies*, before his death on 8 May 1903.

Paul Gauguin,
The White Horse,
1898, oil on canvas, 140 x 91.5 cm

Comparison of works

A legacy which gave rise to a commotion: Caillebotte's legacy, 1897

In 1876, Gustave Caillebotte, aged only twenty-eight, deeply affected by the premature death of his brother René, drew up a will stating his wishes for bequeathing his collection of Impressionist paintings which he had begun to build up: "I bequeath my collection of paintings to the State; however, because it is my desire for... these paintings to neither end up in an attic nor in a provincial museum but rather in the Musée du Luxembourg and later the Louvre, a certain period of time needs to have passed before executing this clause to give the public time to accept, and I do not necessarily mean understand this type of painting. This period of time may be twenty years or more; until that time, my brother Martial or, in his absence, another of my heirs will look after them." When he died in 1894, his collection, made up of sixty-seven pieces, was considered a nuisance, a "complicated business" by the government. The Musée du Luxembourg, which then housed works by living artists, ought to have accepted this legacy. However, having become the preserve of official art over the years, it did not favourably view the possible arrival of the collection, and shielded itself behind some rule or another for not accepting the legacy as it stood. Three years of negotiations were necessary before thirty-eight of the sixty-seven paintings were finally hung on the walls of the museum, applauded by some and booed by others. In 1897, the inauguration meeting unleashed even more feeling: "It is a despicable, shameful den, all those representing painting here, with the exception of two or three, are feeble." The twenty-nine other canvases, which were returned to Martial Caillebotte, would be dispersed by his widow in 1908.

Pierre-Auguste Renoir, *Dancing at the Moulin de la Galette,* 1876, oil on canvas, 131 x 175 cm, 3rd Impressionist Exhibition, 1877

Claude Monet, *Saint-Lazare Railway Station,* 1877, oil on canvas, 75.5 x 104 cm

Claude Monet, *Regatta at Argenteuil,* circa 1872, oil on canvas, 48 x 75 cm

Camille Pissarro, *Kitchen Garden and Trees in Flower. Spring, Pontoise,* 1877, oil on canvas, 65.5 x 81 cm

Édouard Manet, *The Balcony,* circa 1868-1869, oil on canvas, 170 x 124.5 cm

Claude Monet,
The Rocks of Belle-Île: the Wild Coast,
1886, oil on canvas, 65 x 81.5 cm

Camille Pissarro,
Red Roofs, Corner of the Village, Effects of Winter,
1877, oil on canvas, 54.5 x 65.6 cm, 3rd Impressionist Exhibition, 1877

Pierre-Auguste Renoir,
Woman Reading,
circa 1874, oil on canvas, 46.5 x 38.5 cm

Paul Cézanne,
Farmyard in Auvers,
circa 1879-1880, oil on canvas, 65 x 54 cm

Paul Cézanne,
L'Estaque, View of the Gulf of Marseille,
circa 1878-1879, oil on canvas, 59.5 x 73 cm

Edgar Degas,
Woman Getting out of the Bath, circa 1876-1877, pastel on monotype, 16 x 21.5 cm, 3rd Impressionist Exhibition, 1877

Edgar Degas,
Dancer sitting down, leaning forward, massaging her left foot,
circa 1881-1883, pastel, 62 x 49 cm

Alfred Sisley,
The Regatta at Molesey,
1874, oil on canvas, 66 x 91.5 cm

Henri de Toulouse-Lautrec

"Sir, you would be doing me a great service if you came to my studio to pose for a portrait"

Henri de Toulouse-Lautrec,
Louis Bouglé,
1898, oil on wood,
63 x 51 cm

"Sir, you would be doing me a great service if you came to my studio to pose for a portrait. It will probably not look like you, but that is of no importance." This is what Toulouse-Lautrec would say when he spotted a figure which interested him, according to his cousin Gabriel Tapié de Céleyran, and the painter added: "The expression must prevail over the figure." Through full-length or head-and-shoulder portraits, portraits transformed into scenes of modern life, Toulouse-Lautrec endlessly sketched his contemporaries. Paul Leclercq, one of the founders of *La Revue blanche*, who was in his close circle of friends, related: "I above all understood the tremendous ease with which he worked when he painted my portrait... For at least a month, I went regularly to avenue Frochot [where the artist's studio was situated] three or four times a week, but I precisely remember not having to sit for more than two or three hours in all. As soon as I arrived, he asked me to strike a pose in a huge wicker chair... He then looked at me through his eyeglasses, screwed up his eyes, took his brush and, after having had a good look at what he wanted to see, he did a few light brushstrokes on his canvas using very thinned down paint... "That's enough!... Far too nice outside!" Then we would go out for walk in the neighbourhood." This account places the painter from Albi at the opposite extreme to Cézanne, whose models had to pose absolutely still for hours on end. Furthermore, in many of his portraits painted using spirits on cardboard, Toulouse-Lautrec above all attempted to capture meaningful attitudes and blatant facial expressions, the diluted material giving his painting the energy of a quick sketch, like in *Woman with Black Boa*. It was with this painting that the artist posthumously entered the Musée du Luxembourg, having said himself with a combination of derision and modesty: "If I had been blessed with slightly longer legs, I would never have taken up painting."

Henri de Toulouse-Lautrec,
Paul Leclercq, founder of
La Revue blanche, 1897,
paint mixed with spirits on cardboard,
54 x 67 cm

Henri de Toulouse-Lautrec,
Justine Dieuhl,
1891, paint mixed with spirits on cardboard,
74 x 58 cm

Henri de Toulouse-Lautrec,
Woman with Black Boa,
1892, paint mixed with spirits on cardboard,
53 x 41 cm

Félix Vallotton

The "foreign Nabi"

Félix Vallotton,
Moonlight,
circa 1895, oil on canvas,
27 x 41 cm

Félix Vallotton,
The Gods at the Théâtre du Châtelet,
1895, oil on cardboard re-mounted on wood,
50 x 62 cm

Born in Lausanne, Félix Vallotton (1865-1925) arrived in Paris in 1882, where he entered the Académie Julian. He showed his first paintings in 1885, and began his *Livre de raison*, in which he methodically listed his paintings until his death. He became a painting restorer to earn a living. He met Toulouse-Lautrec and Vuillard, took up woodcutting and received commissions from magazine publishers both in France and abroad. He thus became the chief illustrator for *La Revue blanche* published by the Natanson brothers, who attempted to make their magazine the mouthpiece of the avant-garde. On that occasion, he became better acquainted with the Nabis, joining them in 1892, becoming a friend of Vuillard and Bonnard. The "foreign Nabi", on the lookout for all sorts of technical experiments, was equally skilled in woodcutting and painting, moreover the first skill probably influenced the second. He simplified forms to the extreme, handled the planes as masses and reduced volume to bands of colour, treating his subjects without indulgence, sometimes giving them an almost disturbing character. "He feasts only on bitterness", Jules Renard observed in his *Journal*. In *The Ball*, the silhouette of the child preceded by his shadow, running after the minuscule red ball, seems lost in a space without a horizon, too vast to be reassuring. Like in *The Gods at the Théâtre du Châtelet* in which rows of largely unoccupied seats also give an impression of emptiness, the perspective is distorted. In 1899, his marriage to the daughter of an important picture dealer, Alexandre Bernheim, allowed him to penetrate the circles of the upper middle classes which he nonetheless criticised virulently. His painting then moved away from the Nabis heading towards a cold, strange Realism.

Félix Vallotton,
The Ball or Corner of a Park and Child Playing with a Ball,
1899, paint mixed with spirits and gouache on cardboard glued onto wood, 48 x 61 cm

Félix Vallotton,
Dinner, Effects of Lamplight,
1899, oil on wood, 57 x 89.5 cm

Giovanni Boldini and Jacques-Émile Blanche

Literary, fashionable Paris

Jacques-Émile Blanche,
Portrait of Marcel Proust,
1892, oil on canvas, 73.5 x 60.5 cm

Giovanni Boldini,
Mme Charles Max,
1896, oil on canvas, 205 x 100 cm

"He held up his head, so joyously and proudly crested beneath the tuft of his slightly thinning hair, his neck movements more supple, more proud and more flirtatious than other human beings, that faced with the half-human, half-animal admiration and curiosity which he inspired, one would wonder whether one was indeed in the Faubourg Saint-Germain or the Jardin des Plantes." This sarcastic portrait, taken from *À la recherche du temps perdu* by Marcel Proust, was inspired by Count Robert de Montesquiou-Fezensac, a "delightful decadent", arbiter of elegance in the world of the Belle Époque, a symbolist writer and aesthete. Staring at the knob of his walking stick, his hair carefully waved, with an aristocratic if not arrogant or snobbish air, he was brilliantly painted by Giovanni Boldini (1842-1931) in 1897. This painter from Ferrara, who settled in Paris in 1872 and was a great friend of Degas', became the portraitist of the Paris smart set, inventing a kind of living, sensual, non-indulgent portrait, in refined colours, very different to the dignified, noble portraits painted by official artists. When Robert de Montesquiou received his magnificent portrait, he wrote: "My dear Boldini, one of Shelley's characters... found himself face-to-face with himself one day while walking in his garden. The same thing has just happened to me, but even better since the other me that I met bears your signature." With Jacques-Émile Blanche (1861-1942), another society portraitist, who painted Marcel Proust whom he met in 1891 in Trouville, Giovanni Boldini reveals the brilliant, elegant "turn-of-the-century" atmosphere of the Parisian salon society at the end of the 19th century.

Giovanni Boldini,
Count Robert de Montesquiou,
1897, oil on canvas, 160 x 82.5 cm

Henri Rousseau, know as Le Douanier Rousseau

From a civil servant to a painter

Henri Rousseau, known as **Le Douanier Rousseau,**
War or The Ride of Discord,
1894, oil on canvas, 114 x 195 cm,
Salon des Indépendants, 1894

Henri Rousseau (1844-1910) was not, strictly speaking, a "Douanier" or "customs officer": thus christened by his friend, the controversial writer Alfred Jarry, but was simply employed by the Octroi, the government department then in charge of collecting taxes on goods entering and leaving the capital. A mediocre student, he left the provinces for Paris, became a civil servant and came late to painting, like Gauguin. His conciliatory superiors allowed him to set up his easel during his working hours, and he thus began painting the landscapes in front of him – it was only in 1893, having taken early retirement, that he was at last fully able to devote himself to his passion. He was over forty when he began, in 1886, exhibiting each year at the Salon des Indépendants, where his canvases regularly attracted much mirth. However, Pissarro and Signac noticed this eccentric, who had learned neither to paint nor draw, who simplified forms, ignored perspective and struggled to draw figures in luxuriant vegetation. Although the public and critics practically spent their time deriding his work, and his life had been marked by hardship, he never lost hope or doubted his pictorial direction. This is demonstrated by the autobiographical statement that he wrote in 1895: "He has continued to develop in the original genre that he has made his own." He was, in fact, original, and the official painters

Henri Rousseau, known as **Le Douanier Rousseau,**
Portrait of a Woman,
circa 1896, oil on canvas, 198 x 115 cm,
Salon des Indépendants, 1896

Henri Rousseau, known as **Le Douanier Rousseau,**
The Snake Charmer,
1907, oil on canvas, 169 x 189.5 cm,
Salon d'Automne, 1907

he so admired could not give their approval to a painter who had no experience of drawing or perspective, and who handled his subjects using large flat colours. The Impressionists were also unwilling to accept a painter who showed not even the slightest interest in the variations in light: his landscapes were motionless and his figures stilted. However, at the end of the century, he was admired by a fair number of important avant-garde artists: Delaunay, Kandinsky and Picasso.

Comparison of works

The Nabis and the portrait

Édouard Vuillard,
Mme Adrien Bénard, wife of the first chairman of La Compagnie du métropolitain, 1928-1929, oil on canvas, 114.5 x 102.5 cm

Pierre Bonnard,
The Composer Claude Terrasse and Two of His Sons, circa 1902-1903, oil on canvas, 94.5 x 77.5 cm, Salon des Indépendants, 1903

Édouard Vuillard,
Jeanne Lanvin, circa 1933, oil on canvas, 124.5 x 136.5 cm

The Nabis produced numerous portraits which, in most cases, may also be described as genre scenes: reading newspapers, working at a desk, family reunions. Their models were often members of their own families, portrayed among their furniture or engaged in some commonplace activity. Bonnard thus painted his wife, and also his sister Andrée and brother-in-law, the composer Claude Terrasse, his old army friend, and their children. The Nabis also painted their friends and relations, among whom their clients and dealers had an acknowledged place: the Bernheims, the Polignacs, the Natansons and many others. The Bernheim family, for example, had particularly strong links with the Nabis: in 1899, Vallotton married a daughter of the Bernheim family; in November 1907, Bonnard's first personal exhibition was organised at the house of the Bernheim-Jeune family, inaugurating a long series of exhibitions; and in 1913, Vuillard helped decorate their Bois-Lurette property. Friendship and business were combined in an environment in which dealers and painters, chief editors and writers mingled, as in the home of Misia and Thadée Natanson, who often welcomed the painters into their house at Valvins, close to where Mallarmé lived. The Nabis thus demonstrate the increasing role of dealers, whose importance had become evident since the Impressionists: "Dealers have their merits, whatever one says, since the Medicis died...", Renoir declared a few years previously. He added: "If the unfortunate painter had been forced to chase after the art lover before the art lover chased after him, he would have starved to death."

Édouard Vuillard,
Romain Coolus,
1906, oil on cardboard, 74 x 68 cm

Pierre Bonnard,
The Bernheim-Jeune Brothers,
1920, oil on canvas, 165.5 x 155.5 cm

Édouard Vuillard,
Thadée Natanson,
1907-1908, oil on canvas, 200 x 200.5 cm

Édouard Vuillard,
Claude Bernheim de Villers, circa 1906,
oil on laminated paper,
68 x 97 cm, Salon d'Automne, 1906

Félix Vallotton,
Mme Félix Vallotton,
1899, oil on cardboard,
58.5 x 50 cm

Félix Vallotton,
Mme Alexandre Bernheim,
1902, oil on cardboard, 48 x 67.5 cm

Édouard Vuillard,
Countess Jean de Polignac,
1928-1930, oil on canvas,
116 x 89.5 cm

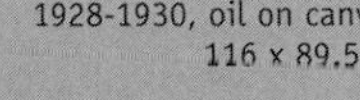

Pierre Bonnard, *The Box,* 1908,
oil on canvas, 91 x 120 cm,
left to right, Mme Gaston Bernheim de Villers,
Josse Bernheim-Jeune, Gaston Bernheim de Villers
and Mme Josse Bernheim-Jeune, in their box at the Paris Opera

The mountains, as perceived by Monet and Hodler

Claude Monet,
Mount Kolsaas in Norway,
1895, oil on canvas, 65.5 x 100 cm

In February and March 1895, Monet, who from the very outset had been interested in studying the effects of snow, decided to visit Norway, since his stepson, Jacques, was living there having married a Norwegian woman. "There are so many different things for me to do which is most infuriating since it is impossible to find more beautiful effects anywhere else. I am speaking of the effects of snow, which are absolutely astounding, but extraordinarily difficult...", he wrote on 1 March 1895. He was particularly interested in Mount Kolsaas, which he painted on several occasions, thus creating a new series of canvases, most of which are in an identical format, with the mountain observed from the same viewpoint: "I am also painting a mountain which can be seen from everywhere and which reminds me of Fuji-Yama. I have had to use six canvases on this latter subject since the effects are so variable, but will I ever see the end of it?" Monet more than likely recognised Mount Fuji from prints by Hiroshige and Hokusai. Here again, it is not so much the subject that he aimed to reproduce, but the feeling he derived from it and which he conveyed in harmonies of mauves, blues and whites. Ferdinand Hodler (1853-1918), a painter of figures, from Bern, also painted many landscapes, particularly of the Alps, which, at the end of his life, he described as "planetary landscapes", and would become increasingly simplified and bare. Like Monet, he had moved away from painting in a descriptive or documentary manner. In *La Pointe d'Andey*, it is the colour which gives the landscape its consistency. "By spending years and years thinking of form, contour and composition, I put colour in second place," he admitted some years later... "Now, I have both, and colour, more than ever before, is not only associated with form, but the form comes alive, and is modelled by colour... I have now discovered large spaces."

Ferdinand Hodler,
La Pointe d'Andey, Vallée de l'Arve (Haute-Savoie),
formerly known as *La Schynige Platte (Switzerland, Bernese Alps),*
1909, oil on canvas, 67.5 x 90.5 cm

Gustav Klimt, Edvard Munch and Vilhelm Hammershøi

Innovators from elsewhere

Edvard Munch,
Summer Night at Aasgaardstrand,
1904, oil on canvas, 99 x 103.5 cm

Vilhelm Hammershøi,
Hvile (Rest),
1905, oil on canvas, 49.5 x 46.5 cm

Although, at the beginning of the 20th century, Paris remained the artistic capital of the world, the rest of Europe was also experiencing new artistic vitality. This was the case for Brussels, but also Vienna, in Austria, where artists wanting to break away from the Viennese Society of Artists, created a Sezession in 1897. Vienna was then becoming the symbol of modernity in terms of architecture and the decorative arts, although painting was not outdone: this is demonstrated by the refined, decorative art of Gustav Klimt (1862-1918), one of the founders of the Sezession and champion of Art nouveau, whose magnificent female allegories often shocked his contemporaries, after the fashion of the disturbing wild imaginings of Dr Freud! His landscapes, rather late in his work, fulfilled no topographical or naturalistic requirements. Often in a square format, and without a background, they rather appeared as flat surfaces with a geometrical design, such as the mosaic in *Roses under the Trees*. Edvard Munch (1863-1944), from Norway, illustrates "mood" painting in which human emotions are of prime importance. Very deeply affected by illness and depression in certain members of his family, he perceived painting as having a moral role, as shown by these words taken from his *Journal*: "One can no longer paint interiors with men reading and women knitting. One should paint living beings who breathe and feel, who suffer and love. Members of the public should perceive that which it shows to be sacred and powerful, and remove their hats, as if in a church." The intimist painting of Vilhelm Hammershøi (1864-1916), also from the North, is at the opposite extreme to Munch's work: greatly inspired by 17th-century Dutch interior scenes and bathed in a silent atmosphere, she conveys moments frozen in time in rather grey monochrome.

Gustav Klimt,
Roses under the Trees,
circa 1905, oil on canvas, 110 x 110 cm

Lucien Lévy-Dhurmer and Odilon Redon

On the edge of reality

Lucien Lévy-Dhurmer,
Woman with Medal or *Mystery*,
1896, pastel, 35 x 54 cm

Odilon Redon (1840-1916) belonged to the same generation as the Impressionists – he, moreover, appeared in their last exhibition, in 1886. However, his painting in no way conformed to the Impressionist style: deeply anti-naturalistic, it delved into a disembodied, spiritual universe. Despite having studied under Gérôme at the Beaux-Arts, this solitary painter mainly taught himself by copying the old masters. He began by trying his hand at etching and lithography, publishing several albums which fascinated Symbolist writers, the titles of which evoked secret worlds of dreams, fantasy and mystery – *Dans le rêve, À Edgar Poe, La Nuit.* Huysmans, together with Gide, Valéry and Mallarmé did not conceal their admiration for Redon's *Noirs* – which is how he himself described his charcoals and lithographs. "To name an object is to suppress three-quarters of the pleasure of the poem which comes from guessing little by little: suggestion, this is the dream." These words written by Mallarmé, the leader of the Symbolists, describe both their poetry and Odilon Redon's art. During the 1890s, Redon gradually abandoned lithography for painting, pastel and watercolour, as he attempted to "open a little door to mystery", as he himself said. At the outermost boundaries of reality, his work announced the discovery of new worlds, the subconscious and dreams. Lucien Lévy-Dhurmer (1865-1953), who was also something of a self-taught artist and had initially trained in a ceramics factory, was a visionary, like Redon. A master pastellist and drawer, he painted evanescent, distant and mysterious portraits. Like Redon, he clearly illustrated the words of Tristan Corbière: "One must paint only that which one has never seen and never will see."

Odilon Redon,
Closed Eyes,
1890, oil on canvas, 44 x 36 cm

Lucien Lévy-Dhurmer,
Medusa or *Raging Wave,*
1897, pastel, 59 x 40 cm

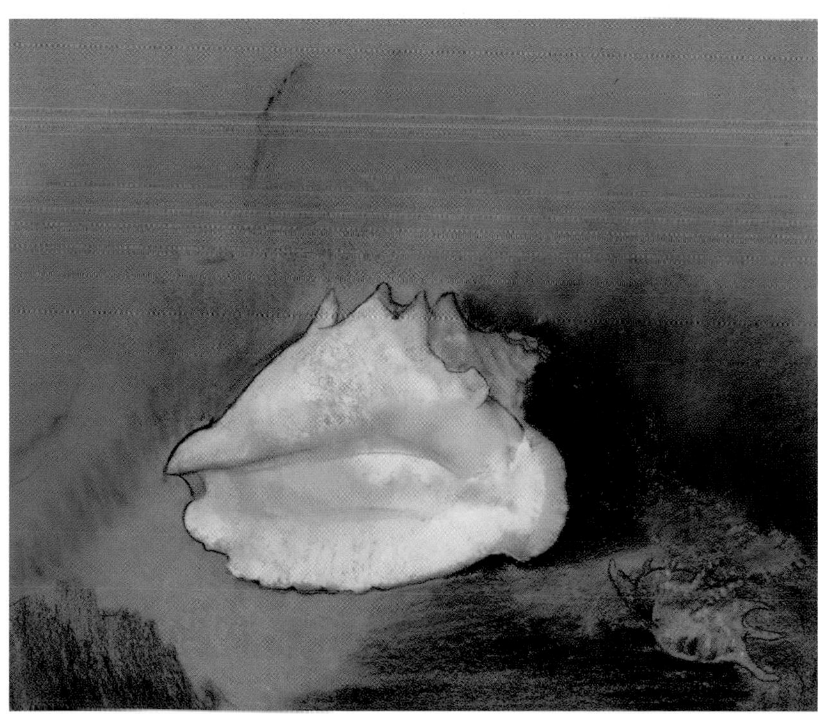

Odilon Redon,
The Shell,
1912, pastel, 51 x 57.8 cm

Comparison of works

The two patriarchs of Impressionism, Pierre-Auguste Renoir and Claude Monet

Pierre-Auguste Renoir,
Gabrielle with the Rose, 1911,
oil on canvas, 55.5 x 47 cm

Pierre-Auguste Renoir,
Young Girl Sitting, 1909,
oil on canvas, 65.5 x 54.5 cm

Pierre-Auguste Renoir,
Mme Josse Bernheim-Jeune and Her Son Henry, 1910, oil on canvas,
92,5 x 73,3 cm

Pierre-Auguste Renoir,
Large Nude,
1907, oil on canvas, 70 x 155 cm

Pierre-Auguste Renoir,
Woman at Her Toilet, Woman Combing Her Hair, circa 1907-1908,
oil on canvas, 55 x 46.5 cm

The first was aged sixty-nine in 1910, and the second aged seventy; the first would die in 1919, and the second in 1926. Renoir's and Monet's careers thus continued well into the 20th century, while painting underwent several "revolutions", such as Fauvism and Expressionism in 1905, Cubism in 1907, and shortly afterwards abstract art. Monet painted Giverny again and again, particularly his water garden which he had completely developed: "My garden is my finest masterpiece." He thus began designing and painting a decorative series totally inspired by the surface of his pond. "I am engrossed in my work. These landscapes of water and reflections have become an obsession. It is beyond my ageing strength, yet I want to convey that which I feel. I destroy them… I start again… and I hope that with so many efforts something will come out of it", he wrote to Geffroy on 11 August 1908. In his old age, Renoir never ceased to pay homage to the most important theme of his career, woman. "A breast," wrote Renoir, "is round and warm. If God had not created woman's breast, I do not know whether I would have become a painter." He thus produced numerous female nudes which he painted in warm colours with flowing brushstrokes which caused them to melt into the landscape. In 1908, he declared to an American painter: "I arrange my subject as I see fit, then I move further away and I paint it, like a child. I want a red to be resonant so as to reverberate like a bell, if that is not the case, I add reds and other colours until this effect is achieved. I am no cleverer than that. I have neither rules nor methods… I look at a nude, I see myriads of minuscule shades. I have to find those which will make the flesh on my canvas come to life and resonate."

Claude Monet,
The Artist's Garden at Giverny,
1900, oil on canvas,
81 x 92 cm

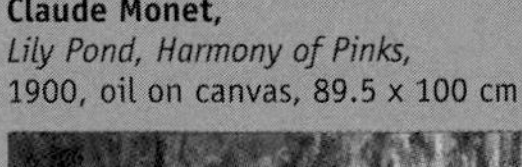

Claude Monet,
Lily Pond, Harmony of Pinks,
1900, oil on canvas, 89.5 x 100 cm

Claude Monet,
Blue Water Lilies,
circa 1916-1919, oil on canvas,
200 x 200 cm

Claude Monet,
London, Parliament; Sun Breaking Through the Fog,
1904, oil on canvas, 81 x 92 cm

Claude Monet,
Portrait of the Artist,
1917, oil on canvas, 70 x 55 cm

Claude Monet,
Lily Pond, Harmony of Greens,
1899, oil on canvas, 89 x 93 cm

Henri Matisse, Maurice de Vlaminck and André Derain

Between Neo-Impressionism and Fauvism

André Derain, *Charing Cross Bridge,* circa 1906, oil on canvas, 81 x 100 cm

Signac had considerable influence at the turn of the century and, during the summer of 1904, Matisse visited Saint-Tropez. In *Luxury, Quietness, and Pleasure*, the title of which was inspired by Baudelaire, he admittedly used divided brushmarks, but took a number of liberties pointing to his later work: the outlines around the backs of his bathers foreshadow the flat colours that he would soon use. Although this canvas also owes a great deal to the large decorative compositions by Puvis de Chavannes and Henri-Edmond Cross, it also draws on Ingres and his arabesques distorting the bodies – in this case, relating to the bather brushing her hair in the right-hand side of the painting. From the following summer, having moved to Collioure to be near Derain, Matisse escaped the tyranny of the small dots. At the Salon d'Automne that same year, with painters such as Manguin, Vlaminck, Rouault, Camoin, Van Dongen, Marquet among others – many of whom had met in Gustave Moreau's studio –, he exhibited canvases with saturated tones which caused a new scandal: the critic Louis Vauxcelles, who noticed a small sculpture in the style of the Florentine Renaissance in the middle of the canvases, exclaimed: "the ingenuousness of this bust is astonishing among this orgy of pure colour: Donatello among the Fauves [or wild beasts]!" The word was spoken, and the term "Fauve" would give birth to the expression Fauvism describing these canvases, "a pot of paint thrown in the public's face", according to another critic. The Fauves would never form themselves into a closely knit group: they rather tended to work in pairs – Derain and Vlaminck in Chatou, Braque and Dufy in the South, Dufy and Marquet in Normandy... – and carried out similar studies at roughly the same time: pure colour applied in vivid flat expanses, free from all naturalistic constraints, creates space, giving rise to great expressive intensity.

Henri Matisse,
Luxury, Quietness, and Pleasure,
autumn-winter 1904,
oil on canvas,
98.5 x 118.5 cm,
Salon des Indépendants, 1905

Maurice de Vlaminck,
Restaurant de la Machine in Bougival,
circa 1905, oil on canvas,
60 x 81.5 cm

Index

Only artists whose work has been illustrated are listed.

RMN/Arnaudet : p. 32, 45, 90, 126, 131, 215.
RMN/Bellot M. : p. 206, 216.
RMN/Bellot/Ojeda : p. 82.
RMN/Berizzi J.G. : p. 47, 88, 100, 101, 103, 107, 110, 145, 194, 209.
RMN/Bernard P. : p. 26, 77, 195.
RMN/Blot G. : p. 11, 13, 15, 24, 44, 69, 79, 102, 109, 115, 116, 132, 134, 135, 141, 142, 152, 153, 156, 157, 159, 162, 171, 193, 200, 205, 207, 210, 211, 215, 219.
RMN/Blot G. /Lewandowski H. : p. 69.
RMN/Blot G./Jean C. : p. 11.
RMN/Blot G./Schormans J. : p. 59.
RMN/El Garby M. : p. 218.
RMN/Hatala B. : p. 199, 214.
RMN/Ignatiadis K. : p. 45, 50, 213.
RMN/Jean C. : 18, 80, 91, 97, 121, 126, 130, 131, 163, 167, 178, 195, 208, 211, 212, 215.
RMN/Lagiewski : p. 43, 219.
RMN/Lewandowski H. : p. 12, 13, 14, 16, 17, 19, 22, 23, 25, 27, 28, 29, 31, 33, 34, 35, 36, 37, 38, 39, 40, 41, 42, 44, 47, 48, 49, 51, 52, 53, 54, 56, 57, 58, 60, 61, 62, 63, 64, 65, 66, 67, 68, 70, 71, 72, 73, 74, 76, 77, 78, 79, 81, 82, 83, 84, 85, 86, 87, 89, 90, 91, 92, 94, 95, 96, 97, 98, 99, 100, 101, 103, 104, 105, 106, 108, 110, 111, 112, 113, 115, 116, 117, 118, 119, 120, 122, 123, 124, 125, 126, 127, 129, 130, 131, 133, 135, 136, 137, 138, 140, 143, 144, 145, 146, 147, 148, 149, 150, 151, 152, 155, 158, 160, 161, 162, 164, 165, 166, 168, 169, 170, 171, 172, 173, 176, 177, 178, 179, 180, 181, 182, 183, 184, 185, 186, 187, 188, 189, 190, 192, 194, 195, 196, 197, 198, 199, 200, 201, 204, 208, 209, 213, 214, 215, 217, 218, 219, cover.
RMN/Lewandowski H./Hubert S. : p. 75, 194.
RMN/Neri P. : p. 111, 119, 129, 194.
RMN/Ojeda R.G. : p. 16, 55, 92, 93, 95, 110, 111, 124, 137, 154, 170, 171, 174, 219.
RMN/Préveral : p. 97, 101, 180, 208.
RMN/Schmidt P. : p. 63, 96, 128.
RMN/Schormans J. : p. 8-9, 18, 21, 46, 73, 96, 97, 109, 110, 121, 130, 131, 132, 170, 171, 206, 214, 217, 218.
RMN : p. 10, 20, 27, 30, 48, 60, 80, 83, 85, 89, 91, 99, 109, 114, 126, 127, 130, 131, 139, 168, 172, 175, 181, 191, 202, 203, 210, 218, 219.

Achevé d'imprimer le 5 avril 2012
par Loire Offset Titoulet
Dépôt légal : mai 2012